BORN JEWISH

BORN JEWISH

A Childhood in Occupied Europe

— • —

By

MARCEL LIEBMAN

Translated by LIZ HERON

With an Introduction by

JACQUELINE ROSE

VERSO

London • New York

First published by Verso 2005
© Verso 2005
Originally published as *Né Juif*
© Editions Duculot, Paris 1977
Translation © Liz Heron 2005
© Introduction Jacqueline Rose 2005

1 3 5 7 9 10 8 6 4 2

Verso
UK: 6 Meard Street, London W1F 0EG
USA: 180 Varick Street, New York, NY 10014–4606
www.versobooks.com

Verso is the imprint of New Left Books

ISBN 1–84467–039–2

British Library Cataloguing in Publication Data
A catalogue record for this book is available from the British Library

Library of Congress Cataloging-in-Publication Data
A catalog record for this book is available from the Library of Congress

Typeset in Fournier by Andrea Stimpson
Printed in the United Kingdom by Bath Press

In memory of the victims.

In homage to the Jews and non-Jews whose common struggle snatched away so many of the Nazis' desired prey.

To my children, so that they may feel compassion for the former and be inspired by the latter.

TRANSLATOR'S ACKNOWLEDGEMENTS

My thanks are due to Adeline Liebman for answering my queries and providing further insights into the experiences described in this book. Also to the Belgian centre for literary translators at Seneffe, for its generous hospitality.

Introduction

JACQUELINE ROSE

TOWARDS THE END of his memoir, Marcel Liebman writes: "Questioning corpses is an obsession I shall leave to those for whom it is a vocation. I have no faith in these false dialogues [...] I myself will settle for questioning history." Liebman came relatively late to *Born Jewish*, this intensely personal account of his life as a child in Nazi-occupied Belgium, which was first published in French in 1977. By the time he wrote it, he had written acclaimed studies of Lenin and of the Russian Revolution; he would go on to write about Belgian socialism, a work incomplete when he died.[1] In his obituary of 1986, Ralph Miliband describes him as: "an independent socialist and Marxist, critical both of social democracy and Stalinism in its many forms".[2] Fiercely independent, he never joined any party. But this did not prevent him from leading a life of political engagement which included negotiating with Anwar Sadat in 1967 for the release of hundreds of Egyptian Jews imprisoned after Israel's victory in the Six Day war. And he was an outspoken critic of Zionism. Liebman's life is haunted by the ghosts of his childhood –

---

1 Marcel Liebman, *The Russian Revolution – The Origins, Phases and Meanings of the Bolshevik Victory*, 1967, translated by Arnold Pomerans with a preface by Isaac Deutscher, London, Cape, 1970; *Leninism under Lenin*, 1973, translated by Brian Pearce, London, Jonathan Cape, 1975; *Les socialistes belges 1914–18 – le P.O.B. face à la guerre*, fondation Joseph Jacquemotte, Vie Ouvrière, 1986.

2 Ralph Miliband, "Marcel Liebman", *Socialist Register*, 1987.

notably that of his brother Henri who, at the painful crux of this memoir, was deported to Auschwitz at the age of fifteen. Miraculously, as this document repeatedly attests, Marcel and the rest of his family survived, but the war "corrupted" the peace and left its survivors "stricken". The tribute he pays to his brother, here and in a sense in the whole corpus of his writing, takes the form of a steady refusal to sacralise his death, in favour of the task of the historian – to question and to go on questioning history, so that its traumas never fossilise. History of this kind does not involve forgetting, but nor does it involve "cultivating" the "memory of the harm". Zionism would make the fatal error of claiming to speak for the dead Jews of Europe, affirming Jewish identity as an absolute. For Liebman, the answer to racism is to denounce it, not to flee behind a defensive, self-isolating barrier of being – and being only – a Jew (hence the dedication here to "Jews *and non-Jews*" in their common struggle against Nazism). Amongst other things, this memoir stands as an extraordinary rejoinder to those who insist that Israel is the only, and definitive, answer to the genocide of the Jews.

One way of reading this memoir is as the story of the birth of political understanding. At the outbreak of the war, Liebman took from his father a fervent Belgian patriotism rendered complex, but somehow unmitigated, by the fact that they were a family of immigrant Jews (his father, born in Warsaw, had arrived in Antwerp as a young child, his mother, born in Oświęcim–Auschwitz, had lived in Zurich before marrying in Brussels at the age of thirty). As children they had been taught to hate communism "which we confused with a rejection of patriotism and a casting out of God". They abhorred Germany and fascism while being "totally ignorant of its nature". As the net closed around them, no teacher at the school spoke of the war. When the announcement was made expelling all Jews, there was not a word of comment or protest. We were treated, writes Liebman, like "frail, blind, befuddled children". Knowledge was "dead knowledge", a "blackening out" of political thought. While the horrors of the war unfolded, there was a "surfeit of talk about the great principles of morality" as "mass graves were being dug and filled". Liebman's indictment of "bourgeois humanism" could not be more severe and it extends beyond the war. When Marcel returns to the school in 1945 with his younger brother, only one teacher notices, let alone remarks on, the fact that Henri, the eldest of the three, is no longer there. At the time, writes Liebman, this "cold passivity", or "fatal resignation", which he now sees as "aberrant", struck him as perfectly natural: "the misfortunes of the war, including the most monstrous forms of racism, never did provoke my indignation at the time".

And yet, there are moments in this account when we can see the kernel of political consciousness. In one striking anecdote from the time of Belgium's capitulation to the Nazis, the roof of the house in which the family were temporarily sheltering collapses. Although several occupants are smothered or emerge to be torn to shreds by shrapnel, all the Liebmans survive. For his father, this is proof – one he will appeal to for years to come – that their family has been chosen by God. For Marcel, such a God – who spares and destroys so indiscriminately, who saves his brother only to send him to Auschwitz – can only be capricious. And what kind of God, as his father-in-law will later insist in quarrels with his father, would save one family while sacrificing another to such misfortune? There is something cruel in the idea of being chosen. Liebman's sense of social justice, and his critique of a too assured Jewish identity, are inseparable. The germs of his socialism and his mistrust of Zionism are simultaneously born.

Near the end of his memoir, Liebman imagines his reader asking him "What does it mean to you now to be a Jew?" For Liebman, there can be no simple or straightforward – above all no absolute – reply. But if Zionism is one reason for his caution, this narrative also offers another in the dreadful story it relates of the part played by the Jewish Councils, or *Judenrat* as they are more famously known, in the deportation of the

Belgian Jews (their role was essential in making those deportations voluntary). *Born Jewish* could be fruitfully read alongside Hannah Arendt's *Eichmann in Jerusalem* of 1963, whose account of the Jewish Councils' complicity with the Nazi genocide has frequently been dismissed or disbelieved.[3] Liebman's memoir fleshes out Arendt's report with the lived substance of this complicity as it rebounds on the painful, if only partially grasped, experience of a young child. Although only five per cent of Belgian Jews had full citizenship, the committees were made up predominantly of Belgian Nationals. Status, class and, it turns out, ethnicity are all decisive. These privileged, bourgeois Jews of Belgium despised the recent Jewish immigrants from Poland whom they saw as another caste: "Well, well!", one of them says to a poor Jewish woman with feeble command of the French language, "If you ended up in Eastern Europe what would be wrong with that? [...] You'd just be going back where you came from!" In this, as Liebman points out, the Belgian Jews were in harmony with their German counterparts many of whom believed that Nazism would only be directed towards the lower orders and that they themselves would be spared. Among the most chilling parts of this memoir are the diary extracts of one "S.V.", a prominent member of the Council, who welcomes the instruction from Berlin to "clamp down on the Jewish problem" ("It seems to be just a matter of mixed marriages. In one sense that would be quite fair"), while lovingly detailing his trips to the opera and consumption of lobsters, as the Jews all around him were being deported or just struggling to survive: "Let us try to be just as happy in the new peace." On the eve of liberation, as he senses the coming recriminations, he dismisses the Jews he betrayed as "high and mighty [...] 'foreigners'" who "have to be put in their place", "jealous ones who've had a bad time of it": "Does it need to be spelled out that [they] are the Jewish survivors of the genocide?" Liebman is unsparing. None

---

3   Hannah Arendt, *Eichmann in Jerusalem – A Report on the Banality of Evil*, New York, Viking, 1963.

of these leaders are ever brought to trial or publicly condemned. When S.V. dies years after the War, he is still "one of the most prominent leaders of the Jewish community in Brussels". To the justification offered by one of their number – that old wounds should not be opened, that the Jews had suffered enough – Liebman simply asks: "Which Jews?"

"In this book", Liebman states after reporting the facts as known of the death of his brother, "I have not asked any questions about myself." It is true that this is not a work of introspection – although its force as narrative is no less for that. But the question of his brother's death is, decisively, Marcel's own question. And in the answers he provides to it, we can see taking shape the personal and political vision, the terms of analysis, or the outlines of what – as historian and socialist – he was subsequently to become. "Preserved from any social consciousness", "taught fervour but not lucidity", Henri died first out of ignorance, a befuddled blindness which passed from the national consciousness into the schoolroom, depriving the children of this tragic generation of the tools for understanding, let alone resisting, what was happening to them. But he also died as the victim of murderers and their numerous accomplices among the European bourgeoisie which had armed fascism, and then "gazed without turning a hair" at the "tortures inflicted on the Spartakus league in Germany, on the miners of the Asturias, on Guernica and on the German proletariat".

This moment in the memoir is something like a clarion call or political manifesto. It also has the profoundest relevance for us today. The issue, then as now, is not just the most glaring atrocities at which we can all be comfortably outraged, but the wider, often hidden, net of implication and complicity. For Liebman, understanding Nazism leads inexorably to the most basic truths of social inequality and exploitation under capitalism. To that extent, his brother is the victim of a murderous Nazism riding the back of a class system, whose deadly ramifications are simply exposed at their most treacherous by the behaviour of the notable Belgian Jews.

While there is no limit to the ingenuity of his father in saving most of his family from the worst of fates (the book is also a tribute to his "cleverness and clear head"), nonetheless, for the most part, you died in occupied Belgium if you had neither the money, privilege nor connections with which to protect yourself. S.V. is no aberration; he is representative. Death becomes a matter, not just of the race or caste, but also of the class into which you are born: "If being Jewish was the worst of misfortunes, the plight of poor Jews brought them even closer to total strangulation and utter doom." Class distinctions were at once "respected and reinforced" by the war: "The fact that I was a child masked these distinctions from me, but it did not protect me from them."

It is one of the strengths of his memoir that Liebman can be so unerring in this analysis while at the same time acknowledging the point where understanding trails off into uncomprehending terror, where the most painful part of mourning trumps all rational thought. "Against all reason", Liebman will strive to "give solidity" to this brother for the rest of his life; he will struggle for an "elusive and ungraspable" knowledge that – the more he reaches out for it – "disintegrates" in his mind.

Towards the end of the war, Liebman is sent to the town of Schaltin where, on condition of disguising their Jewish identity to the other inmates and masquerading as Spaniards, he and a number of Jewish boys are taken in by the *Jeunesse Ouvrière Chrétienne*. This was one of many organisations sponsored by the Catholic Church that played a huge part in securing the lives of young Jews. Behind this move was the hand of the *Comité de Défense des Juifs*, a Belgian resistance organisation, which is one of the heroes of the book. Resistance is key to this memoir. It is the other face of Liebman's preoccupation, not only with the fate of his brother, but also with that of his cousin, Maurice. Henri dies because he takes a detour to visit a young woman on his way to the Town Hall to collect ration cards for some Jewish friends too afraid to venture out, instead of arriving at the crack of dawn when the Gestapo were less vigilant. But Maurice, in a gesture as brave as it is futile, gives himself up to the Nazis in order to join his recently captured parents and brother. Why? For Liebman, such "poignant passivity" can be traced to the "messianic dream and exaltation of martyrdom" that the Jews have historically taken from their experience of exile and persecution. He does not judge Maurice; in many ways he admires him. But he is in no doubt that this "profoundly noble and absurdly powerless" response to historical suffering played its part in the horrific destiny of the European Jews by giving murderers "free rein, so that they became the unassailable perpetrators of an inevitable destiny".

To resist is therefore to answer that destiny with the fullest claim for another, potential, history. It is also, crucially, to recognise the affiliation between Jew and non-Jew. The strongest resistance came from the far-left Zionists, the social democrats of the Bund and the communists – the last of the three assuming the most active role. Militants like the communist Gert Jospa, one of the founders of the "Committee for the Defense of the Jews", were men who in their social relationships and political choices were "not particularist Jews cultivating and exalting their differences", but immigrants connected to Belgian working-class organisations, whose rootedness in local and political life, together with their distance from power and privilege, gave them a different sense of what cunning, well-orchestrated, action could do. In the southern industrial city of Charleroi, the Jews joined with the militants of the far left to form the "Jewish Solidarity of Charleroi", and compiled false lists of Jewish citizens for the Gestapo, depriving the Nazis of "hundreds of their prey". At Malines, on the day of the Warsaw Uprising, a group of militants linked up with prisoners in the Dossin barracks to sabotage the twentieth transport of Jewish deportees to Auschwitz.

There is another sub-text here. These moments read like a model for a revolutionary party at once able to seize its moment and organised (if the adventure at Malines had been more organised, they could have saved more). They offer, that is, a type of ideal political action based on a form of discipline that has not yet hardened into bureaucratic power. In his writings on Lenin and on the Russian Revolution, Liebman steers the most delicate course between the need for a revolutionary Party that can take political control, and its inherent dangers (thus although he insists in *Leninism under Lenin* that Lenin was "thoroughly democratic in character" and the "eternal enemy of nationalistic and bureaucratic tyranny", he nonetheless acknowledges that his belief in the vanguard contained the seeds of what was to come).[4] In *Born Jewish*, it is as if we are given flashes of political agency, at once organised and urgent, which – in the intensity, risk and necessary brevity of their moment – are never in danger of corrupting themselves. Against such moments, the privileged Jews of the *Judenrat* are like a Party cut off from its base. Nor did any of the more traditional Jewish institutions, who proudly displayed "the Jewish label in terms of either nationalism or religion", come anywhere near such achievements. They were all trapped by a social isolation they chose for themselves and which "the Nazi occupier criminally aggravated and exploited": "The heroism of the Jewish partisans, acting in concert with non-Jewish partisans, is sufficient proof that it is not lack of courage which explains the passivity of the majority, but their marginal situation in Jewish society."

There is an important history here. For Liebman, the disaster that befell Belgium in the 1940s must be traced back to the German occupation of the First World War, when socialism was sacrificed to patriotism, and previous links between socialists across national barriers crumbled in the face of a new militant nationalism. We only have one part of Liebman's second volume of his history of Belgian socialism, but it is a remarkable document that is in some ways the companion volume to, or hidden history of, the work published here. Before the war it had been

---

4 Marcel Liebman, *Leninism under Lenin*, p. 425, p. 433.

possible to see capitalism as inherently belligerent – "capitalism," as Jaures once put it "brings war like a cloud brings the storm".[5] But once the war was cast as the struggle of an innocent victim against an external aggressor, then all such analysis, together with any critique of the state as answerable for the horrors of war, was lost. In Belgium, the left flocked to the service of the "sacred union" of the nation; of all the socialist parties of Europe, the Belgian Workers Party – this is the fundamental reproach of Liebman's study – were the most complete in their capitulation to this ideal. "All differences of opinion, all disagreements, all divisions" were suppressed and the nation became a family united "in its hatreds" by a "mixture of triumphalism, euphoria and the will to revenge".[6] Belgium entered a time warp and "the entire political life of Belgium was numbed by the fact of the occupation".[7]

The worst ill, therefore, is self-idealising patriotism, or "sacred egoism", a form of butchery since it justifies sending thousands of young men to their deaths.[8] Above all, this form of patriotism – which saved some of its harshest penalties for any fraternisation with enemy troops, while repressing the most graphic reports from the front – is a form of ignorance and isolation. Patriotism destroys thought. As they will be again in 1940, the Belgian citizens of 1914 are cut off from the forms of knowledge and understanding they need most. This is therefore far more than just a plea for the workers of the world to unite. It is at once a denunciation of pure nationalism, and a lament for what might have been other more generous forms of affiliation. In this account of Belgium as "martyr country and innocent nation",[9] it is impossible not to discern a powerful analogy with Liebman's critique of Zionism –

---

5 Liebman, *Les socialistes belges*, Jaures cited p. 4.
6 Ibid., p. 14, p. 52.
7 Ibid., p. 67.
8 Ibid., p. 57.
9 Ibid., p. 61.

remember that the "exaltation of martyrdom", as enshrined in Jewish history, was seen by him as playing a central part in his cousin's embrace of death. But it is also more than an analogy. In his writing on 1914, some of Liebman's harshest criticism is reserved for nations such as France and England who, even as they claimed democracy as the objective of the war (which would of course be the war to end all wars), were busily carving out new worlds "whose contours remained shrouded in the densest mystery".[10] Israel will be one of the legacies – the Balfour declaration, allowing for the creation of a Jewish homeland in Palestine, is issued in 1917 – the product of colonial omnipotence, and national grandiosity, steadily eroding the possibility of European socialism, and shadowed by the horrors of war.

For Liebman, Zionism is therefore colonialism, but it did not have to be. After an episode of fervent Jewish spirituality at Schaltin (he even briefly contemplates becoming a rabbi after the war), he is gradually alienated from the rigidity of traditional Judaism which he feels enclosing around him after 1945, only to return to Jewishness "through the roundabout route of politics". By then he is living in England, and, hugely influenced by Ralph Miliband, is a Marxist. Alienated by the excesses of Stalinism, he eventually takes up the cause of Arab–Jewish rapprochement in the context of the Algerian war. A joint struggle against French colonialism might offer the new Israeli nation a model for co-operation between the two peoples and unharness the new state from the West. What appals him right to the end is the unconditional support for Israel which he feels paralyses so many Jews; nor can he accept the demand Israel makes of all Jews to go to Palestine, an exodus which, in his mind, "uproots", and "maims" and "leaves the field to the enemy". Jewishness must find itself in the connections between peoples, whether in the diaspora or in Palestine.

10 Ibid., p. 36; on 1914 and its effects on international socialism, see also Liebman, "1914: The Great Schism", Socialist Register, 1964.

To the end of his life, Liebman maintains these positions, while argu-
ing for justice for the Palestinians. He does so undaunted even when, in
public, he is shockingly compared with the worst of Belgian collaborators, accused in the room where his father died of precipitating his death
(in fact, without sharing them, his father had defended his son's political
views), and even of betraying his brother: "How can you attack Israel
and defend the Palestinians? Don't you think of your dead, your own
people, your brother?" "On the contrary," he concludes, "I think of
them very much." For Liebman, the best tribute he can pay his brother
is to acknowledge that, in killing him, racism hacked out a void that
cannot be filled. Not by statehood, nationality, or race – false icons of
our times. The greatest danger is to "beam" "the blinding lights of
yesterday's conflagration" onto the children of today. "Leave my children – and yours", he pleads, "to follow their own inclinations." Finally
Liebman's appeal is for a Jewishness not sealed behind walls of conviction, but open to the infinite possibilities of tomorrow.

Jacqueline Rose
June 2005

I

ON 1 SEPTEMBER 1939, late for a war (like those older and less naive than me), I tore off to a Brussels barracks in the hope of seeing our young conscripts as they left to defend the frontiers of the kingdom with flowers on their rifles and joy in their hearts. I was ten years old and in my memory were bygone images from *Illustration*.[1] At Place Dailly, however, I saw nothing resembling the enthusiastic scenes that had occurred twenty-five years earlier around the Gare de l'Est in Paris, and I went home disappointed.

These too were days when people waited impatiently to know whether France and Great Britain would send help to Poland, now under German attack. Friday 1 September passed without bringing any declaration of war by the Western Powers against the Third Reich. Nor did this come on Saturday 2 September. Finally, on Sunday the 3rd, at 11 am precisely, Chamberlain reached a decision and announced that his country was now at war with Germany. Nonetheless, in the early afternoon, when I set off for the Sunday show at the cinema with my brothers – Henri, aged twelve, Léon, eight, and Jean-Claude-Albert, who was three – France had not yet joined its ally. Impatience gave way to anxiety. Two hours later, as we left the "picture house", a wireless boomed

---

1 The French illustrated paper (Trans.).

out of a nearby shop, repeating news broadcast earlier: Daladier had followed Chamberlain's example. What a relief: war at last! War had finally come, with its procession of glory and heroism; war and the imminent fall of the Nazis.

A few weeks later, we saw for the first time a different face of war – real war. My mother had a sister in Poland, at Oswiecim, a town that was to become famous under its German name: Auschwitz. When the first news reached us, and with us other Jews, my mother started getting parcels ready. I remember my surprise when, along with a few clothes and some tinned food, she put in a single shoe. The other one was added to a second package sent soon after. I was told that this was a precaution to stop the Germans from stealing these shoes. They wouldn't be able to make any use of just one. What about the clothes and the tins, I asked my mother, what was to stop them from helping themselves to those?

Letters arrived from time to time, censored of course but for all that making things plain enough. My mother read them in tears. In one of these my aunt confided that she would like to be with one of her female relatives – someone we knew was long dead. We also heard that in Poland Jewish women were forced by the SS to clean the pavements on their knees, with their skirts. This seemed far-fetched, but was very worrying. And yet the war continued to inspire us with the same military fervour.

At first, with what verged on a relish for battle, we had followed the Poles' frenzied resistance on the Westerplatte, which we believed was halting the German offensive. And, with equal rejoicing, the first push by French troops, an advance of a few kilometres into the Saarland, without the least idea that this toehold would soon get bogged down in the blunderings of the phoney war.

And so as that summer ended and autumn began, those were exhilarating times. But then excitement began to wear off. We imagined we were reliving the epic days of 1914–1918, whose patriotism had sustained us. This was the patriotism of official ceremonies and school displays, a

The Liebmans at the Bois de la Cambre in Brussels (1933).
From left to right: Marcel, Léon, the cousin who had been "taken in",
the boys' mother, Henri, and, on the right, one of the author's uncles.

patriotism which was first and foremost one of the main ideological components of the atmosphere at home. What a strange and extraordinary situation for a Jewish family of recent immigrants. My father, born in Warsaw, had arrived in Antwerp when he was still a young child, while my mother, born in Oświęcim–Auschwitz, had lived in Zurich for a long time before getting married and settling down in Brussels, when she was nearly thirty. So we could easily have been like tens of thousands of Jews who throughout the 1930s lived in Belgium in many respects as outsiders to Belgian society, forming circles of German Jews, Polish Jews, Dutch or Romanian Jews, in full awareness of their otherness, their standing and condition as foreigners.

For them, there were numerous obstacles to integration. There was the language, which in Antwerp, the great "Jewish metropolis", was particularly complicated by the fact that here Flemish was spoken. The émigrés who settled there had little inclination to learn it, and the reasons for this reluctance were no mere matter of philology, since Yiddish was much closer to Flemish than to French. But at that time French was still the language of the bourgeoisie and thereby a vehicle for upward social mobility. The Flemish people also had two characteristics which discouraged any tendencies to familiarity and integration: they were still for the most part peasants and deeply Catholic. More generally, the Jews of Belgium had often viewed this country as no more than a staging-post on the journey towards the main centres of attraction in America. Added to this was a crucial economic factor: Jews were often concentrated in specific professional sectors, and at Antwerp especially in the diamond industry. This reinforced their cohesion. The majority had practically no knowledge of a Belgian society which held few attractions for them. In this respect there was a substantial difference between them and Jews who had settled in France. Whether brand-new immigrants or otherwise, the latter saw their host country as the homeland of the Rights of Man and a centre of prestigious culture. In Belgium, however, where the national question remained unresolved, the lack of any ethnic homogeneity and the absence, beyond a relatively small circle, of any patriotic consciousness, heightened the Jewish immigrants' sense of being distinct. The economic difficulties of the 1930s, compounded by feelings of mistrust or hostility towards foreigners, saw to it that the Jews became locked into their judicial, social and psychological condition as displaced persons.

But we didn't regard ourselves as foreigners. We felt Jewish, but Belgian: Jewish *and* Belgian. Jewish through our ancestry and through a religion whose rituals we practised and which made us "different": different, for example, from our school fellows, because, on Saturdays, though we went to school, we weren't allowed to do any writing. This was deemed a sensible relaxation of our religion's prohibition against working on the Sabbath.

Finding the Belgian homeland in a German POW camp.
The author's father is on the extreme right.

We would listen with total attention, but the old ancestral creed –
albeit adapted to the requirements of life in the West – would paralyse
our hands. Every year the teacher would be made privy to some of the
secrets of the Jewish rite and would take note of them without any reser-
vation. But one Saturday my teacher was away. His replacement gave
me and my classmates a dictation. He viewed me with surprise: "Why
aren't you writing?"

"Because."

He wasn't satisfied by my answer and kept on. I stubbornly refused
either to reply or to write. The awkwardness of the situation and the
embarrassing silence were a mark of our semi-integrated state and our
marginal status: we were different from other people and, though a little
ashamed of it, determined to remain so.

In this we resembled countless Jewish children. But, unlike the great
majority of them, we felt ourselves to be no less Belgian, indeed
intensely Belgian, with the kind of patriotic fervour which nowadays is

inconceivable. We owed this fervour to my father. He was an extraordinary character; he was legally stateless, Jewish by his ancestry, by his
religious observances and by sundry attitudes and traits of character –
yet, for all that, in his heart he was Belgian. By chance, he had happened
to be in Germany at the beginning of August 1914 and had declared
himself a Belgian citizen rather than a Russian.[2] This had earned him
more than four years in a camp for political prisoners deported from
Belgium to Germany. With his perfect knowledge of German, his considerable ingenuity, and a flair for organisation matched by a highly
energetic sense of duty, he had become one of the camp leaders. Having
been more or less abandoned at the age of twelve when his father got
married again, to a young woman who begrudged her stepson any affection, and having lived in the most utter poverty, this little Antwerp Jew
rubbed shoulders in that prison camp with some of the sons of the
Belgian grande bourgeoisie – among them the young Paul-Henri Spaak
– and even a few aristocrats who had honoured him with their admiring
and grateful friendship. In a book published between the wars about the
experience of Belgian prisoners in Germany, *Z, lettre de misère*, the
author, Furquyn d'Almeida, had turned my father into the main hero of
his story, seeing in him an archetype of the prisoner who is canny but not
self-interested, energetic but incorruptible.

In Belgium he had never known the warmth of a family home; in
Germany he discovered the warmth of camaraderie. Those years of
imprisonment – for the "cause of Belgium" – were the best of his life.
He came out of the war a patriot and, by virtue of his association with
the youthful elite of Belgian society, he emerged a conformist and a
conservative. He was so patriotic that the day after the armistice (which
found him at the head of a camp of tens of thousands of prisoners) he
"re-enlisted" to serve in the Belgian espionage networks in Germany.

---

2 He was born in Warsaw and on this basis counted as a subject of Tsar Nicholas II.

After several years of activity, he was arrested by the Germans, getting himself a heavy sentence and a fresh incarceration. He came out of this even more of a patriot. In my fullest and clearest memory of him from my childhood years, I can see him polishing up his decorations just before going off to some patriotic ceremony, or else at one of these, a severe and solemn figure invariably next to the national flag.

One day, during one of the festivities organised by the Jewish religious community of which he was a member, he managed to have the "Brabançonne" sung, the Belgian national anthem – by a congregation usually impervious to its (frequently disparaged) beauty. For him, this was truly a grand triumph. However, one young man nearly dampened his jubilation by blatantly refusing to stand during the singing. My father didn't think twice: he slapped the young whippersnapper as everyone stood by dumbfounded. He took all the more pride in this absurd and vengeful action because the culprit was the son of a banker from whom the community derived certain material advantages and a good deal of prestige. As far as my father was concerned, conformity did not rule out a readiness to challenge. When it came to his conservatism, this turned him into an assiduous reader of the French right-wing press. Heaven knows how, he even put up with Gringoire and Candide. Their anti-Semitism wounded him deeply, but his attachment to patriotic values gave him the wherewithal to forgive them.

Through a lawyer friend of his who was attracted by Rexism,[3] he agreed to give talks in those circles where pro-German collaborationism was to recruit a great many of its adherents. My father hoped to give these energetic and xenophobic partisans of the right proof of the greatness of the Jewish people and the pointlessness of their anti-Semitism.

He was a foreigner, but the family background that had rejected him never ceased to matter. For a long time he had lived in a poverty which

---

3 The Rexist Party was a Belgian political party of the extreme right, fascistic in type, led by Léon Degrelle.

set him even further apart from it, so he pathetically looked for a way of rehabilitating himself by mixing in Belgian milieux which were willing to admit him and where, moreover, he bought his way in: in the war veterans' association which he partly ran a song went round which had the chorus "It's always Liebman who foots the bill!"

His children were equally patriotic. And this anachronistic virtue which I have long since dispensed with is something I am glad to have drawn some benefit from. For, unlike the majority of my Jewish peers of those days and later on, I have never felt foreign in the country where I live and which, ever since childhood, I became accustomed to seeing as my homeland. I was well aware of the existence of Palestine, "Eretz-Israel", because my father's conformity managed to conjoin with the same emotion his love for Belgium and his scarcely less ardent, albeit paradoxical, love for the "Zionist project". I was well aware that on the far side of the Mediterranean there were Jews like us who had their own country, that they were its pioneers and were even – a wondrous thing! – soldiers. Was this my country too, despite my already having one: Belgium? Would I some day have to get to this country and leave my land of adoption? This ghastly dilemma was resolved at the time since for some reason I was afraid of the sea and storms, so a trip to Palestine was ruled out. I would therefore stay in Belgium and this was just as well. In any case, I shall never have the slightest difficulty in seeing the Belgians as my compatriots. My solid sense of rootedness owes more to my father's patriotic convictions than to an accident of birth or my own considered thinking.

Moreover, we were well aware that ours was an unusual and exceptional situation. My father had drawn the contempt of his Antwerp family upon himself; they reproached him with the preposterous and shocking notion of spending so much time with "goyim". And my brothers and I too, we spent time with them, without a second thought, without it ever bothering us. Certainly, we did sometimes find ourselves involved in extremely unpleasant incidents. "Filthy Jew!" is an insult I have heard more than once, although it has never been addressed to me personally. In such circumstances, all I could do was go to the aid of the insulted (my brothers often, since they got more than their share of this) and give free rein to my pugnacious temperament. It didn't strike me as being very important. In the face of all logic perhaps, I continued to believe that it was in Germany that anti-Semitism raged, and in far-off Poland where Jewish women cleaned the pavement with their skirts.

II

WITH THE INVASION of Belgium by German forces on 10 May 1940, the war was upon us. Though its onset had sent us into a puerile and jingoistic state of exaltation, these sentiments did not withstand the first disappointments.

Just as in September 1939, I soon realised that the great patriotic scenes of 1914 would not be repeated. Around the Gare du Nord in Brussels, which I had rushed to, almost by second nature, on the morning of 10 May, the warmth of that wonderful springtime filled the air but not our hearts. We found our consolation in the martial tunes that boomed out from the radio and the unforeseen delight of the school closures that followed the start of hostilities. There was no trace of anxiety in our minds, even that evening when, thanks to an incursion of German planes over Brussels, we had to go down into some cellars that had been hurriedly, and even symbolically, turned into air-raid shelters. Thus we began to play at war in earnest.

The next day, the unexpected encounter with our first British military lorry reinflated our enthusiasm. "They're heading for the front!" – as once to the Marne, to Verdun or the Chemins des Dames. But on Sunday 12 May the front began to get closer to us. My father, though resolved to maintain a civic optimism to the very end, showed signs of agitation. He left for Antwerp to see his father and his family again and to involve

them in contemplating a departure which might one day prove necessary. He established only that the majority of his relatives, not least his
father, had waited for neither his visit nor his advice and, without bothering to let him know, had already set out on the road to exile. He
considered their haste to be excessive and their silence humiliating.
Being in such a great rush betrayed a very reprehensible defeatism, yet
for some of them it was wisdom itself, for after a few weeks of wandering hither and thither they found their bearings again in America.

   In the days that followed, my father made an increasing number of
secretive approaches to the friends he had in high places. These flatter-
ing connections (he was always fixated on being the "little Jew"
honoured by the good opinion of his betters), which he had maintained
for many years with his former fellow prisoners, had more than once
been of use to German Jews who had illegally taken refuge in Belgium,
often to become the beneficiaries of a parsimonious hospitality. There
were, for example, those Oppenheimers, whose harrowing visits I can
recall. My father's insistent pursuit of the matter with a high-level functionary in the Belgian Sûreté finally bore fruit and one day the
Oppenheimers came to tell us that their situation had been regularised.

   Nevertheless, my father was not always so fortunate in his approaches.
His friend Liekendael spoke to him about his difficulties. A very long
time after, I was able to deduce the nature of these problems. It was
revealed in an extremely rigorous work of history published in 1971,[4]
that the head of the Belgian Sûreté, Monsieur De Foy, who was arrested
by the Germans shortly after the invasion, was straight away released
thanks to the intervention of the notorious SS commander Heydrich.
Heydrich stated that, in the course of the phoney war, this Belgian
police officer had supplied his colleagues in the Gestapo with extremely
valuable files. What is more, I found out from the researches undertaken

---

4 Jules Gérard-Libois and José Gotovitch, *L'An 40, La Belgique occupée*, Brussels, Crisp, 1971.

by a young academic (with supporting original documents) that this collaboration between the Belgian security services and their Nazi counterparts had existed since 1933, its aim being to organise the hunting down of communists as well as to keep an eye on the Jews, whom the Belgian police suspected of being the authors of anti-Nazi graffiti on the Antwerp–Aachen train.

So as not to aggravate the level of unemployment, which in any case had been in gradual decline ever since 1935, and not to upset the Belgian right and extreme right any further, or else, more simply, out of indifference, the government displayed an extreme reluctance to welcome the victims of Nazi persecution, whether these were left-wing militants or refugee Jews. Only particularly tragic cases could induce them to soften this attitude. One of these had the result of enlarging our circle of friends.

Monsieur Schönberg was a Viennese Jew who, together with close on a thousand "citizens" of the Third Reich, had obtained the right to leave Hitler's Germany. On board the steamer *Saint Louis*, their misadventures in the spring of 1939 earned them the biggest front-page headlines in the newspapers. The émigrés were in possession of a Cuban visa which authorised them to disembark in Havana. A propaganda campaign organised by German agents who had infiltrated the Caribbean induced Cuba to withdraw its agreement. The plan hatched by the Nazis had succeeded: it demonstrated that they were not alone in opposing the Jews, that other states deemed them equally undesirable. With its contingent of refugees whom no one wanted, the *Saint Louis* was forced out of the Havana docks. The United States refused them a visa and the ship turned away from the American coast en route for Germany. On board there were acts of desperation: suicides and attempted mutiny. In the end, a number of governments were moved to share the thousand-strong German and Austrian Jews between them. Around 300 disembarked in Belgium, a provisional haven where their persecutors would find them again a year later.

On 13 and 14 May, my father took steps that for once had a self-interested goal. He sought to obtain authorisation to leave Brussels for
France in a train reserved for civil servants and their families. This
authorisation was won by dint of a significant struggle; after all, my
father did not have Belgian nationality and his foreign identity card did
not favour his efforts. On 15 May, early in the morning, the family left
the house, not without a squabble breaking out between my father, who
was hurrying everyone along, and my mother, who could not resign
herself to giving up her home without having washed the dishes. So we
were heading off towards exodus! With a total of 600 francs in our
meagre kitty, a derisory sum for two adults and four children. The fact
was that since the spring of 1939 we had become impoverished. My
father was the Belgian representative for a Czech firm and he too had
been a victim of the Nazi entry into Prague, since the occupation of
Czechoslovakia by the Germans cut short his regular professional activity. From then on, and throughout the war, he had to keep coming up
with different ways of earning a little money. He managed this only with
great difficulty and very skimpily. At all events, he never allowed himself to be compromised, either directly or indirectly, in the black market,
and when, in autumn 1940, he succeeded by some miracle in getting hold
of a few dozen hams and a similar number of Camemberts at a "pre-
war" price, he distributed most of them among his friends without it
having crossed his mind to make any profit from them at all. Was it
because of this unfailing altruism that my brothers and I had to go
hungry – and sometimes very cruelly – throughout all those years of
hardship?

On 15 May, at 7.30 in the morning, we were put on one of the last
trains to leave Brussels before the arrival of the Germans. This was a
convoy of cattle trucks, which made us no less aware that we were
enjoying a signal privilege. The fact that we owed it to our father further
reinforced the admiring trust which we placed in him at that time. For

my part, I maintained this trust throughout the whole course of the war.
Thus in my eyes my father embodied strength and wisdom; I never
doubted the rightness of the decisions which he took upon himself without ever consulting any of us – my mother least of all. With hindsight
and for all sorts of reasons, this wisdom now strikes me as more than
doubtful. I believe that the blind trust which surrounded him masked a
mixture of naivety, impulsiveness and powerlessness which ultimately
disarmed us in the midst of upheaval.

The 16 May, however, brought us fresh proof of my father's infinite
powers. It was nearly thirty-six hours since our train had left the capital.
Thirty-six hours of desultory travel across the Flemish countryside on a
journey broken up by countless halts and numerous bombardments. In
the vicinity of Ghent we accordingly spent a night of terror, our first. In
the early morning, the train set out again, en route for what we thought
was France, in other words safety. It seemed plain to us that German
troops would never set foot on French soil. This may have been because
the Franco-Belgian frontier would appear to them as an insurmountable
strategic obstacle, or a symbolic line that it would have been sacrilegious
to cross; it was irrelevant. Once we were in France we would be safe. My
father had struck up a friendship with the mayor of La Madeleine, a suburb of Lille. This high-placed person would certainly have no trouble
getting us to Paris. Fuelled by our store of memories – literary ones by
now – we asked ourselves which lycée we would go to: Louis-le-Grand
or Condorcet, to pursue highflying studies, and for how long? The main
thing in the end was to reach Lille.

Unfortunately, the train was proceeding very slowly, and when we
got to the little station of Langemarck, not far from Ypres, it ground to
a complete halt. An announcement was made that it would go no further.
France, and safety, abruptly seemed out of reach. My father, however,
disappeared without telling us where he was going. He wanted only "to

try something", he said as he left us. An hour or two later, a sumptuous black automobile drove along the platform and stopped when it came to our wagon. My father got out of it: the car was for us! In a few words my father explained that the *bourgmestre* of Langemarck had put it at his disposal, because he was a Jew, a First World War political prisoner and, to boot, sentenced by the Germans for spying. Beneath the astonished gaze of the other refugees, we piled into the limousine. In order to leave the station, it backed up a long way, then it abruptly stopped and didn't budge. It had broken down! But what of it; my father left us there, went off to find his *bourgmestre* again, told him about his troubles one more time, touched his heart accordingly and came back to the station with a different but hardly less luxurious car than the first one. Off we went again, this time heading for Lille.

Neither Lille nor the French frontier were ever reached. After some fifteen minutes on the road, our driver noticed how late it was, remembered that a curfew had been imposed by the authorities and decided to make tracks back to Langemarck. He gave us an appointment for the following morning at dawn. But that was the day the Belgian military command put a ban on civilian traffic on the roads. My father made another attempt to get us to France by settling on an exorbitant price with a peasant who took us in his cart; but the latter had to make do with an IOU since my father didn't have the wherewithal to pay him. He set us down near Poperinghe, close to the French frontier, at a farm which took us in for a few days. Enough time for my father to get hold of a vehicle that would take us to Lille. Finally he found a car and I can remember that short journey which I imagined was my route to exile: "I'm leaving my country, deserting my homeland" – I kept telling myself this with tears in my eyes. My nostalgia was premature and quite superfluous into the bargain, since when we reached the frontier post we were driven back by the French because we were stateless persons to whom entry was forbidden. A few hours later, sick at heart, we went back on foot along the road we had travelled that morning, returning with despair to a country I had thought I was leaving with sadness.

The days that followed were doubly extraordinary: because of their tragic intensity and also because they turned us into refugees like everyone else, subject to the same dangers and a prey to the same anxieties. In the whole of the war this was the only point when our condition as Jews was obliterated. Chance brought us to a small Flemish village in the immediate vicinity of the French frontier, where there was a junction of different roads leading to Dunkirk. As we later realised, this particular circumstance was what brought about the hardest trial to be endured in that month of May. In the final days preceding the Belgian Army's capitulation, this area was the target of a constant bombardment that became more and more deadly with the progress of a German Army which though still invisible was horribly present. It was then that I truly discovered the fear of death, of an immediate death – in the cellars of farms where we found refuge and where the noise of the explosions was accompanied by the voices of women reciting interminable "Hail Marys". We had a sense of being in a pit from which we would not be able to escape.

Early in the morning of 29 May, a rumour went around which struck us at first as unbelievable and then as scandalous: the Belgian Army had capitulated! We scarcely had a chance to comment on this event. The little house where we were staying was by the side of a road taken by the last French units leaving Belgium. My father decided to ask for their protection, but he had less luck than with the *bourgmestre* of Langemarck. The officers whom he stopped had no inclination to listen and even less to take civilians in tow. I can still see my father coming back into the house, discouraged for the first time and for the first time aware of his total powerlessness.

The catastrophe hit us moments later. With a horrifying crash, amid the noise of explosions, the roof suddenly collapsed and the house was filled with blinding dust. "Everybody outside!" my father shouted.

Everyone dashed out onto the road. In a matter of seconds we found ourselves in a field, face down, jammed into the ground, while the shells whistling about robbed us of any desire to raise our heads. My father was there, my three brothers and an old woman. And where was my mother? ... She had disappeared. When my father realised, he got up and headed towards the house, which was now in ruins. At this moment my mother appeared in a door frame, along with a young woman. A fraction of a second later the young woman collapsed in a pool of blood; a shell or a piece of shrapnel had just blown off both her legs. One of us began reciting the "Shema Israel", the most solemn prayer in the Jewish liturgy, and this was quickly taken up by the others. Suddenly, the old woman who was beside us got up and was immediately struck down; she was only a few yards away from me and her body was now no more than a sponge with streams of blood flowing out of it. She was screaming. My father tore off towards the road to try and stop the French soldiers and get them to bring help to the wounded woman. None of them would stop. Within minutes she was dead from loss of blood.

The morning's reckoning was a heavy one. Some fifteen refugees occupied the house, four families in all, including ours; each of these families had at least one casualty. Mine was the only one to have escaped. Three dead and a number of wounded were pulled from the rubble. We thought of our survival as miraculous. My father retained this conviction until the end of his life: God had protected us. This frequently repeated statement was often met with a twofold rebuttal. Mine was inspired by a reflection of simple common sense: so who was this capricious divinity who protected us in May 1940, in particular saving my older brother in order to allow his deportation and his death in Auschwitz a few years later? Whereas my father-in-law, who had a fiery temperament and a deep sense of justice, would fly off the handle any time my father brought up the "miracle" of 29 May in his presence. How could anyone imagine a God so unjust that he could accord the safety of his protection to one family while sacrificing the others to misfortune? For all that, my father never conceded the point and remained persuaded that our lives on that day had been personally protected by God.

It took a few days to recover from the shock, and a few days too for us to remember that, despite everything, we were not the same kind of refugees as everyone else. We only had to see the first German soldiers to become aware of this again. For several days, the family wandered along roads overflowing with streams of civilians. It was no longer a matter of us waiting for a limousine or any other kind of vehicle to come to the rescue. In any case what use would it have been to us? We knew that the Germans had entered France, eschewing scruples or respect. Lille had probably been occupied already; our retreat was cut off. We would have liked to make our way home, but we had no choice in the matter so we made do with following the crowd in the hope that people would gather at assembly points where someone would take care of getting them back. So this was how we found ourselves stranded on the Belgian coast, in a little seaside town we had known in the happy days before the war, although nothing there was reminiscent of the peacetime past; everywhere there were refugees, everywhere there were ruins and rubble. ... Everywhere too there were German soldiers. I remember the first I saw: they were motorcyclists, their appearance made even more frightening by their goggles. Around us, everyone was staring at them with curiosity, especially the children. We, however, were panic-stricken, suddenly horrified, and then as if instinctively, without a word being said, my brothers and I made a move to hide our noses. The giveaway nose, the suspect nose, the Jewish nose.

We had become Jews again, wretched indeed just like millions of other refugees, worn out with tiredness just like them, hungry like them, but with a different kind of wretchedness.

We received confirmation of this a few days later. In a vast square at Ypres crowded with lorries, thousands of men, women and children had gathered to wait for the Germans to see to it that they were returned home. In groups of thirty, they were piling into lorries heading for the main Belgian cities. We sat on the ground eyeing one another in puzzlement over whether to accept this help from the Germans or not. And would our refusal be a matter of dignity or of prudence? For the first time, I saw that my father was uncertain. So uncertain that he went so far as to ask our advice. My mother categorically opted for going back, with or without dignity. And what about prudence? ... Well, what did we have to lose? ...

Half an hour later, we were on a German truck, the speed of it going to our heads. What a difference from the woefully slow train that had taken us away from Brussels a few weeks earlier! And we were so fascinated by the extraordinary spectacle around us that it made us feel a kind of elation. Everywhere, there were troops on the march, and heavy artillery, demonstrating the efficiency of an impeccable war machine. Right then we had almost forgotten that those proud, smiling faces were those of our enemies, that their elated singing celebrated our defeat and announced our misfortunes. So we went on through Menin and Courtrai. It was in Ghent that this journey came to an end, when a German officer took the opportunity to come up to us in the course of a halt.

"*Sind Sie Juden?*" he asked my father.

"*Ja,*" my father answered.

"*Raus!*" came the officer's laconic retort.

Within seconds we found ourselves standing in the road at Ghent.

The Occupation had begun in earnest. And while the time of persecutions had not yet started, nor that of the yellow star, we had by now become acquainted with discrimination, and were already marked out.

III

THE END OF 1940 and the year that followed were uneventful for us. We had settled into the war, which is to say into hunger. There would come a time when the problem of hunger would strike us as laughable. Until the summer of 1942, however, when the persecution of the Jews began in earnest, what concerned us most was the business of getting hold of food.

As I said, my father had lost his job in the spring of 1939, and he still refused to turn his hand to the black market. He had to make do with the meagre rations allocated by the official food supply services, eked out only by the resourcefulness of a mother who had been confined, ever since her marriage, to the strictly limited sphere of household chores.

Not long ago, a friend happened to come across two photos of my mother in a family album: one taken when she was around thirty years old, the other twenty-five years later. It was a tragic contrast that revealed a woman completely exhausted by life. The countless forms of misogynist conservatism combined with a Jewish cultural tradition that reduces women to nothing more than wives and mothers had ultimately turned her into a nonbeing, living in the shadow of her husband and of serving him, in the shadow of her children and entirely devoted to them; more than – or less than – obliterated; negated in a personality which she had finally surrendered.

One last summer without history (August 1941).

Added to social conditioning were the random events of her own life. After arriving aged thirty in a country where she knew no one and didn't speak the language, in order to marry a man whom she had to learn to love, she had withdrawn into the family home and had quickly become isolated by her role as nothing more than wife and mother. Four pregnancies had worn her out. Motherhood had claimed her completely. "Above all she's the mother of my children," my father would say, imagining that with this he was paying her a compliment.

In a period when we were living in great poverty, for a number of years she had been saddled with the additional demands of looking after a young cousin. The child of divorced parents, he had been placed by his mother in the care of a non-Jewish working-class family. My grandfather had considered it sacrilegious that his grandson should be brought up by "goyim" and he put pressure on my father to assume responsibility for the child. My father did not dare refuse; my mother, already over-whelmed with chores, gave way under this extra burden. Isolated and reclusive, subjugated by a husband upon whom she depended in every sense, and who ultimately crushed her by the force of his personality, she lived in Brussels like an exile until the day she died.

Her real homeland was Switzerland and Zurich was her Jerusalem. Until the end of her life, she kept drawers crammed full of ribbons, dresses and baubles that dated from the happy days of her youth. Every time we moved house my father insisted that she get rid of this old stuff. My mother, who gave way to him in everything, remained impervious to his injunctions and indifferent to his mockery on this one non-nego-tiable point. She had left Switzerland in 1927 and never set foot in it again. My father went there once with my older brother, but my mother stayed at home. For who would have taken care of the children? Even the idea of seeing Zurich again probably never occurred to her; it was a dream beyond the reach of a woman whose fate was incarnate as wife-object and mother-servant.

One afternoon in October 1960, she lay down on her bed after lunch. Without taking enough time to recover from her tiredness, she cut short her nap to go off on some household errands.

"Rest a little while longer," one of my brothers told her.

"No, duty calls." These were her very words.

They were her last words. Fifteen minutes later she was hit by a car. She died that same evening.

During the war, committed to the duties of the miracle worker, she ful-filled this role without the least self-congratulation, nor the slightest gain in her standing or authority. For all that, and for all that she did, we frequently experienced hunger, in particular my older brother Henri and myself, and we resorted to any number of ways and means to make her feel better. Often, we would make bets with food as a stake: for example,

half of a meal. The loser then had to make a show of being full in order
to justify the act of transferring the greatly coveted leftovers to the win-
ner's plate. On other occasions, we would plunder my father's little library
and secretly sell some books, and with the money from the sale we would
buy fruit or pastries. One day, however, Henri made a discovery – in one
of the big food shops on Boulevard Anspach they were selling large dishes
of ice cream that was probably not quite fresh. The price was reasonable,
even with the addition of the fares required for these expeditions that were
secret but all the more wonderful for that. Last of all, in the fine weather,
shamelessly if not fearlessly, we would steal potatoes by uprooting them
from the fields around Brussels. My mother made no objection and my
father closed his eyes to it. Alas, the owner of the field just beside the rifle
range, where we carried out our raids, kept his wide open. This enraged
peasant caught us red-handed, and while I managed to make a run for it,
my elder brother was dragged off to the police station where he got away
with a severe telling-off and his pledge that he would never do it again.

He kept his promise and I followed his example. Or rather, I shifted
the sphere of my illicit activities. I abandoned my rustic pilfering and
specialised in urban expeditions enacted in the arena of the department
stores in the Rue Neuve. I lifted what were sometimes extraordinary
quantities of "classroom items": bound exercise books, coloured pencils,
pens, compasses, etc., all of them marvels which our classmates possessed
and which we cruelly lacked. I operated on my own, expecting nothing
from my brothers except their encouragement – which they supplied in
abundance – and their discretion. My talents and my growing audacity
allowed us not merely to impress everyone in the classroom where before
we had been ashamed of our appalling school equipment, but also to
build up a reserve for the future. It never occurred to us to sell any of
these items. My predatory activities lasted a few weeks longer, until the
day when a floor manager caught me in the act. He took hold of me, but
I managed to get free of his grip, tore out of the shop and ran for twenty

One bar of chocolate between four. (The author's grandfather and his second wife in 1942.)

inches wide that was just enough to cover the bottom of my legs. My shoes – or what was left of them – would then cover up the nakedness of my feet, and my honour was saved.

Pastimes and entertainments also suffered in the hardships of the war. Although we didn't lack for books, thanks to the public libraries, we could no longer think of going to the cinema. We found it harder to accept not being able to see football matches any more, since we were big fans, so we continued going to sports grounds without ever having an entrance ticket to our names. It wasn't just the entrance to the stadium that was beyond our means, but the, albeit modest, cost of public transport. We had to walk all the way to football grounds that were sometimes very remote. At best we would be given enough to pay our fares there or back and we would get home exhausted. I remember one particularly sorry Sunday when I had to carry my little brother on my back because his shoes were too small for him to be able to cope with our eight-mile forced march. Of course, there would come a time as yet unsuspected when all these troubles would strike us as paltry compared with the permanent insecurity, the frequent dread, the dispersal of families and our uncertainty about the fate of those who were closest to us. During the first years of the war, however, all these different privations weighed heavily on us and I have no doubt that in some manner or other they left their mark.

By way of compensation, we had the warmth of a home where harmony greatly prevailed along with a profound sense of camaraderie, especially among the children. Never did this warmth seem so great as on Friday evenings, when we celebrated the start of the Sabbath. The weekly ritual was supremely reassuring, for it gathered us together in an atmosphere that was often happy and always comforting. There was hardly ever an event, however cloudy, that the fervour of the Sabbath – particularly on Friday evenings – failed to brighten up. The prayers and the singing played a great part in this, but also, I confess, and perhaps to a larger degree, the more nourishing meals, the more generous portions and the particular dishes that were more filling, more varied and more apt to smell good. That evening, we dispensed with our bets and we went to sleep with full stomachs. Then all we had to do was count the days until the Friday after, the next oasis in our crossing of the desert.

It soon became clear to us that this crossing was going to be a long one. We had never doubted, however, that victory would finally fall to the side of democracy and freedom. This conviction which in 1940, and even in 1941, was more a matter of faith than of wisdom, was fuelled somehow or other by the rare reversals encountered by the Germans. Our hopes hung on each event that held back, all too briefly, the interminable round of their victories. I remember that day in May 1941 when the radio gave us news of Rudolf Hess's landing in Scotland. I can clearly remember my delight when I went to school that afternoon. I had the feeling that the war had reached a decisive turning point, that the Nazis recognised the impossibility of invading the British Isles and that this confession of impotence was going to be their downfall. It was the first good news since the catastrophes of May and June 1940. At least that was what we believed for several days. A month later, we had the same illusion when the Soviet Union entered the war. We momentarily expected that the Red Army would put up a victorious resistance against the Germans and hasten the hour of our liberation. All of a sudden we found ourselves liking the land of the Soviets, having always hated it as much as we hated communism, which we confused with a rejection of patriotism and a casting out of God. After 22 June 1941, these cardinal sins seemed to us like venial shortcomings. One of our neighbours was an elderly retired colonel whom we were very fond of because of his good nature and – reason enough – because he was a colonel. He made frequent strenuous efforts to convince my father that it was no good the Russians fighting the Germans – to little avail, moreover – since the Bolsheviks were no less dangerous. I witnessed these discussions, though I don't think they made any contribution to the belated blossoming of my political awareness.

In general, the war fostered strategic thinking (you can easily imagine how clear that was!) rather than political. We abhorred Germany and fascism, but we were totally ignorant of its nature. All we did was plot troop movements on a succession of maps: Libya, Greece and Yugoslavia, Russia. But the lightning progress of the German armies soon wearied our attention. When all was said and done, the war further strengthened a patriotism that was already very intense, but it did not lend itself to any improvement in our feeble political education. Admittedly, our school environment was particularly barren in this respect. I can't imagine any reference to the war being made by a single one of the twenty or so teachers whose responsibility it was to inculcate the rules of arithmetic, geometry, Latin, grammar and history. There was no one, with the exception of a vaguely fascistic music teacher, who extolled the merits of the new order; nor anyone who denounced its fraudulence either. At the same time as the world was split in conflict and the worst form of political thuggery threatened to blank out enlightened thought, there was the most total ideological void.

In the winter of 1941, my older brother, then in his second year at secondary school, took the risk of launching a patriotic demonstration in the classroom on 11 November. We had followed the secret preparations for this as if it were an event of such magnitude that it would shake the power of the Third Reich. On the day in question, at 11 o'clock precisely, all the pupils were to stand and respect a minute's silence, an interminable minute charged with emotion and with anger. Everything went according to plan. Only the teacher remained seated and, once the gesture of protest was over, he resumed his scholarly exposition of the mysteries of geology without a word of comment.

In the teaching of history, which that year concentrated on antiquity, we were given a number of lessons on the Hebrews. Although the kingdom of Israel and the religion of the Jews came up a great deal, the teacher managed to avoid any allusion to contemporary events and the anti-Semitic discrimination which had already been set in motion. At that time in schools it was de rigueur to be totally apolitical, although this was a matter of appearance rather than reality. There was a surfeit of talk about the great principles of morality, but eyes were closed to their daily violation. History had been divested of even the vaguest reference to the world around us, literature of the least mention regarding the works of our own day. There was a pretence of forming young minds in the humanities while remaining silent about the lives of human beings. Along with dead languages, we were taught a form of dead knowledge which was the substance of flabby, spineless teaching. Today's school students ought to know how their counterparts of those crucial years were treated: like frail, blind, befuddled children. Our teachers' lessons were perfectly in keeping with this blindness and they maintained it. It is not as if they were paralysed by fear or by prudence. Their paralysis was inborn, and this was proved by the silence they continued to observe after the war and the Occupation were over, about all the events that had combined to make the ghastly fabric of those years. At a time when mass graves were being dug and filled, they talked about the timelessness of morality. And when these were discovered, they reiterated their phlegmatic speeches, without being perturbed in the slightest.

Here there is a truth that goes beyond issues of education and relates to the bourgeois humanism with which they lulled us right through the "parenthesis" of the war, as if there were nothing untoward going on. Nothing: neither racist slaughter, nor killings in general, neither totalitarianism nor sordid mercantilism, nor the Resistance either, since no one breathed a word about it. The appointed time for speeches came only after the Liberation. And these were still confined to the patriotic ceremonies for which we tirelessly prepared with our lengthy rehearsals of what were meant to be martial processions. Not a single word of explanation was ever given but, by way of introduction to the empty patriotic homilies, there were endless drill exercises where we tried – sometimes successfully – to march in step. We were then ready to render just homage to the war dead and the official authorities. The latter would arrange themselves around monuments commemorating pupils who had died between 1914 and 1918, and between 1940 and 1945. This long list did not include the name of my older brother. My father took steps to have it added, and clashed with the ill-disposed "prefect of studies" who told him that Henri had not died bearing arms. Doubtless, but another "old boy" had been cited on the marble although he had been killed in the course of a bombardment. Of course, but his corpse had been identified. The small war waged between the school authorities and my father continued for a long time and prolonged the big one. As in the latter case, it ended with the triumph of right and justice.

Although Henri had died unarmed and his remains went into a cremato-
rium oven, his name appears engraved on that stone. What is most
strange is that we have always found a kind of comfort in seeing that
mute and eloquent inscription.

Above all, in 1941, the crucial thing was holding on. The Allies *couldn't
not* win the war, and the entry of the United States into the conflict confirmed this certainty. Meanwhile, we had to keep up the struggle against
hunger, and hope that German anti-Semitism wouldn't have the time to
go beyond the framework to which it seemed to have restricted itself in
Belgium, as likewise in France at the time: numerous kinds of discrimination, odious without a doubt, but none of which would accommodate
the intention to come up with a "final solution" to the "Jewish question".
But where we saw signs of relative moderation there was, instead, evidence of devious cleverness. This amounted to allaying the victims'
suspicions while at the same time isolating them increasingly from the
rest of the population, stifling them economically, further diminishing
their capacity for resistance and even all their inclinations to react against
the measures for extermination which were being made ready by stealth.
When the terror was unleashed it would then have the suddenness of an
earthquake, delivering its prey bound hand and foot to the executioners.

How could we guess at the outline of what was later to be called
"genocide", within the totality of administrative measures which were
progressively decreed by the occupiers in relation to the Jews? Early in
the autumn of 1940 orders had been given for Jews to be recorded as
such in the local registers of residents in the Belgian electoral districts,
whose administrative authorities participated willingly in this racist
operation. From then on the identity cards of Jews indicated the origins
of those holding them, in three languages: French, Flemish and
German. This discrimination struck us at least as having the advantage
of being discreet. Less discreetly, the owners of Jewish shops had to

The start of the persecution: "Entry prohibited to Jews". (Photograph courtesy of the Centre de Recherches et d'Études historiques de la Seconde Guerre Mondiale, Brussels.)

place a sign on their frontage carrying the likewise trilingual inscription indicating a Jewish business: "Entreprise juive, Joodsche Onderneming, Jüdische Unternehmung". What is more, from 1940 Jewish lawyers found themselves prohibited from practising their profession and Jewish civil servants, albeit not numerous, were removed from the administration. The Jewish university teachers suffered the same fate. In Antwerp, a significant and in particular a very dense and homogeneous centre of Jewish population, very attached to the specific traditions of the communities of Eastern Europe, from 1940 discrimination assumed more aggravated forms. A large number of families received the order to leave the city and settle in the province of Limbourg. Moreover, Jews were forbidden from entering public parks. Later, in 1941, all the city's Jewish inhabitants had their radio sets confiscated. However, until the spring of 1942, for us life still seemed tolerable. We thought we could – just about – adapt to the presence of the Germans. There were probably a lot of Jews who had already opted for a tougher stance. But that was only achieved by elements of the left. In the general rout that had followed the invasion, these groups alone had remained active: the far-left Zionists, the social democrats of the Bund and the Communists. It was the last of these that would quickly assume the most important role in the most active forms of resistance; out of some 300 "terrorists" shot by the occupiers as hostages, there were precisely thirteen Jews. All of them were connected to the clandestine communist organisations.[5]

All in all, the two years we had just spent under German occupation were reminiscent of the phoney war: a persecution that wasn't quite that, a (very relative) lull that ushered in the dramatic events of summer 1942. In the very last weeks before the summer began two things happened that proved the vice was tightening around us. One day in

5   These hostages should not be confused with the partisans sentenced to death by the Germans. The statistics under this heading are less precise, since they group acts of general resistance together with armed actions.

May, while we were in the classroom, a "supervisor" (someone usually entrusted with strictly administrative duties) interrupted one of the lessons to read out a communication which we thought at first was purely routine. It wasn't. In glacially bureaucratic terms it announced that, from the start of the next school year in September, Jewish pupils would no longer have the right to attend any primary or secondary educational establishments. The reading of this aroused no comment. It might have been announced that the school day would finish a quarter of an hour later or earlier from then on, and the effect would have been the same. I recall no protest, no hint of indignation, nor even just of surprise. Not one of the pupils or teachers felt the need to demonstrate the least feeling of sympathy for my brothers and me, all three of us pupils at this Brussels *athénée*,[6] with its progressive reputation. And when the school reopened its doors to us, two years later, after Liberation, there were only two teachers out of the twenty or more whom we had known during the war who thought of asking us why there were only two of us and what had become of the third. Nor did anyone express their gratification at finding us alive. I can also say that during the war this indifference never shocked me. For some reason that I am no longer aware of and which I now surmise was probably ill-founded, I found this cold impassivity perfectly natural. In general terms, moreover, the misfortunes of the war, including the most monstrous forms of racism, never did provoke my indignation at the time. They aroused a sometimes panicky fear, a sense of total confusion and on occasion of horror and despair. In my family it never struck us that the crime being perpetrated was unnatural, nor that it ought to give rise to feelings – far less actions – of rebellion. I am not proposing to give any explanation here for a fatalistic resignation which I now see as aberrant. It is enough for me to note it and to go on asking myself the reasons for it.

6 In the Belgian education system, the *athénée* is equivalent to the French lycée.

A Jewish man wearing the star at the Old Market. (Photograph by J. d'Osta.)

More or less at the same time the German order was issued compelling Jews to wear the star. My mother had to sew these emblems, which she carefully cut out from a square of yellow fabric, onto the front of our jackets or the bodice of her dresses. The appearance of these stars in the classroom during the final days of the school year provoked no incident. Except that one pupil saw fit to make a remark: "With a nose like yours, you could easily do without your star."

A long time after the war, a Parisian relative would tell me that in his school there had been violent brawls between the Jewish pupils wearing stars and their non-Jewish fellow pupils, as teachers looked on with quite unperturbed indifference. Nothing like this occurred in my Brussels *athénée*. Likewise in this circumstance, the rule of silence and serene detachment was perfectly observed.

Quite by chance, the day on which this apocalyptic summer began, 21 June 1942, my family was celebrating my bar mitzvah, and this solemn celebration of my "religious majority" was the occasion of the reunion which, with hindsight, makes me think of a wake on the eve of a funeral. Besides my parents and my brothers, one of my grandfathers was there, as well as uncles, aunts and cousins whom for the most part I was never going to see again. Along with the photograph of this bar mitzvah, I have kept two other mementos of the occasion: a menu handwritten by my father, its length testimony to my parents' last gastronomic efforts, and, even more significantly, a book of Jewish history – the great classic *Grätz*, in its Hebrew version. This was given to me by a cousin and it bears the following dedication:

At difficult times in your life, you will peruse this book and find in it fresh sources of courage in the existence of a people which has been perpetually overwhelmed with misfortune and has endured these vicissitudes with indomitable pride .... A people that has no wish to die and will never die.

The final family get-together: the Bar-Mitzvah (21 June 1942).

I made a very solemn speech. I was favoured with a great number of liturgical blessings and a somewhat smaller number of presents. I was fortified by the old synagogue chants, which were all melodies whose sound was familiar in the family circle and which were being sung for the last time by so many of us. Thus, quivering with intense emotions, we entered the hurricane. Around the same time, less than 200 miles away, a Parisian Jewish family opted for a less traditional and rather darker ritual route into clandestinity. My brother-in-law told me how, with a sense of foreboding that the end was close for him and his two young boys, his father, a poorly paid rag trade worker in the Sentier clothing district, made up his mind to cut himself off from the world. Scraping together the last of his savings, he decided to allow himself a treat that twenty years of hard work had always put beyond his means. He had bought three tickets for the Folies-Bergères. Not just any seats, but orchestra stalls! The three of them, the poor worker and his sons (aged ten and thirteen), had taken their places, all three of them wearing their yellow stars as required, among the rows of pretty women and German officers. They watched the entire show – an amalgam of cheerful frivolities which they had never experienced before and which, in all probability, they would never experience again. Then, when the curtain came down, they left the hall and headed for a final walk along the grand boulevards, after which they buried themselves in a cellar from which they were not to emerge for another two years, emaciated, gaunt, miraculously alive and scarred for ever.

IV

THE 31 JULY was a memorable date in that unforgettable summer of 1942. For some ten days we had been living in fear and expectation of an increasingly inescapable event: our notification.

Jewish families in Brussels and Antwerp had already been receiving home visits from delegates of an institution set up by the Germans, the famous AJB (the Association of Jews in Belgium), with the task of giving them notification regarding their "assignment for work". This launched the major operation of deporting the Jews of Belgium.

The AJB was established in November 1941 and to begin with confined itself to low-profile activities whose scope was unknown to most Jews. The very existence of this institution went almost unnoticed. In my family, however, the initials AJB had soon become familiar. My father cherished the hope of joining it and he sought appointment to some office of responsibility. He knew the Association's president, Ullman, the Chief Rabbi of Belgium, and he repeatedly brought to his attention the useful role he himself could play, primarily in the negotiations that would have to be entered into with the German authorities.

"I'm a man of action and I know what the Germans are like," my father had declared. "I 'gulled' them often enough during the First World War. They never once got the better of me. I could help you make sure they don't get away with anything."

"Well, you see," the rabbi had replied, "I'm not a man of action and this is not the spirit in which I envisage our work at the AJB."

"What is the spirit you'll be acting in?" my father then inquired.

"It's hard to answer that," said the president of the AJB, "but I'll tell you a little story that will give you some idea of what I have in mind. When I was a young rabbi and I had to leave my native city to come to Western Europe, I paid a farewell visit to one of my relatives, a man of great wisdom and deep piety. This is what he said to me: 'I am too poor to give you a present that would prove my affection for you. Instead I'll give you some good advice. And here it is: whenever you have any doubts about the wisdom or appropriateness of an action, refrain from doing anything.' That is the philosophy to which I always adhere," the Chief Rabbi concluded.

This was the man who had been entrusted with the leadership of an institution designed to play a cardinal role in the dramatic story of the Jews of Belgium. Associations of the same kind had been set up more or less everywhere in the occupied countries. In September 1939, the infamous SS chief Heydrich had called for their establishment, seeing them as a means of carrying out the "final solution" to the "Jewish question". He had specified that such "Councils of Elders" or "Judenräte" should be made up of Jewish notables as well as religious figures. It was this directive that inspired the German authorities in Belgium when they formed their *Judenrat*. The governing committee was appointed by the occupier and headed by the Chief Rabbi. On it were a number of businessmen who for the most part were Belgian nationals, yet scarcely more than 5 per cent of the country's Jewish population had Belgian citizenship, and those who did came from the better-off social groups. The function to be fulfilled by this extremely bourgeois association was very much directed towards the "final solution". For though its articles of association made provision for social welfare activities which the *Judenrat* had to pursue in the overriding interest of those it governed, it was likewise laid down that the new institution had to assume responsibility for "preparing for the emigration of the Jews". What is more, the organisation of charitable works was nothing more than a sham. One of the official documents of the German command at a high level made it plain that the objective was to "lock the Jewish economy in Belgium into a moral ghetto and above all to eliminate it from the country's social life". After that, it would quite clearly be easier to organise the "emigration".

In its early months, the AJB put its efforts into setting up a variety of institutions, primarily in the spheres of education and welfare. Then it got down to serious business. In the first instance, this involved drawing up a new register of Jews, as required by the Germans, updating the one established by the Belgian municipal administrations in the autumn of 1941.

The AJB's local branches in Brussels, Antwerp, Charleroi and Liège accordingly put the details of tens of thousands of Jews on file.[7] This was around the same time when Jews became compelled to wear the Star of David. To begin with the Germans had wanted to make the Belgian municipal authorities carry out the whole operation, but they came up against a refusal. They then turned to the AJB, which complied, though only after questioning the *bourgmestre* of Brussels.

"Why are you refusing to participate in this operation, given that you agreed to set up a special register for the Jewish population in 1940?" asked one of the AJB leaders.

"Because at the time we were still in doubt about whether there would be a British victory," answered the *bourgmestre*.

By June 1942 the Jews' "assignment for work" had begun. This targeted adult males, for whom deportations were organised to the north of France; there they were put to work in appalling conditions on the construction of the Atlantic wall. This preliminary stage seemed

---

7 At the time there were some 22,000 Jews registered in Brussels, 17,000 in Antwerp, 3,000 in Liège and 1,500 in Charleroi. Out of this total, 2–3,000 had Belgian citizenship.

L'Autorité Occupante nous remet ce jour un ordre de prestation de travail établi par elle à votre nom.

L'Association des Juifs en Belgique est tenue de vous le faire parvenir dans le plus bref délai.

D'après les assurances données par l'Autorité Occupante, il s'agit effectivement d'une prestation de travail, et non d'une mesure de déportation.

Prenez soin de vous munir du trousseau prévu sur l'ordre de prestation de travail; dans le cas où certains objets vous manqueraient, vous pouvez vous adresser à l'O.C.I.S., 43, rue Joseph Claes, à St.Gilles-BRUXELLES ou au siège du Comité Local de l'A.J.B de votre agglomération (si vous habitez la province)

Les événements graves des derniers jours nous obligent à attirer votre attention sur le fait que la non-observance de l'ordre de prestation de travail pourrait entraîner de facheuses conséquences, tant pour les membres de votre famille que pour la population juive toute entière du pays.

Vorstand des J.V.B.	**S. ULLMANN,**	Président de l'Association des Juifs en Belgique.
Vorstand der Jundische Kultusgemeinde Brüssel	**M. BLUM,**	Président de la Communauté Israélite de Bruxelles
Vorsitzender des Lokalkomitees Brüssel der J.V.B.	**S. VANDEN BERG**	Président du Comité Local de Bruxelles de l'AJB
Verwaltungschef der J.V.B.	**M. BENEDICTUS,**	Chef de l'Administration de l'A.J.B.
Vorsitzender des Lokalkomitees Lüttich der J.V.B.	**N. NOZYCE,**	Président du Comité Local de Liège.
Vorsitzender des Lokalkomitees Charleroi der J.V.B.	**J. MEHLWURM,**	Président du Comité Local de Charleroi.
Vorsitzender des Hilfswerkes O.C.I.S.	**D. LAZAR,**	Président de l'O.C.I.S.
	R. HOLZINGER,	

Die zustaendige deutsche Behoerde uebermittelt Uns heute einen von Ihr auf Ihren Nahmen ausgestellten Arbeits-einsatzbefehl.

Die Vereinigung der Juden in Belgien ist beauftragt Ihnen denselben auf raschesten Wege zuzustellen.

Zufolge den Uns von der Behoerde gegebenen Zusicherungen, handelt es sich lediglich um Arbeitseinsatz, und nicht um eine Disportationsmassnahme.

Sorgen Sie für Ihre Ausrüstung mit den vorgeschriebenen Gegenstaenden welche auf den Arbeitseinsatzbefehl verzeichnet sind. Falls Ihnen gewisse Gegenstaende fehlen sollten, können Sie sich, in Brüssel, an die O.C.I.S. 43, rue Joseph Claes, St. Gilles-Brüssel, in der Provinz : an die zustaendigen Lokalkomitees wenden

Die bedauerlichen Vorkommnisse der letzten Tage veranlassen uns, Sie darauf aufmerksam zu machen dass die Nichtbeachtung des Arbeitseinsatzbefehles sowohl für Sie als für die Mitglieder Ihrer Familie, wie auch für die gesammte Jüdische Bevölkerung des Landes besonders harte Folgen haben würde.

The notification for Malines.

relatively bearable, but we had an increasing feeling that the noose was being tightened. Late June and the early weeks of July brought a growing sense of oppression. Yet for a large number of Jews the illusion remained that this was just a "bad period". One of my Antwerp cousins took the opportunity to get engaged on the last Sunday in June. He was leaving for the north of France a few days later; from there he would be deported to Auschwitz. His fiancée stayed on in Antwerp but she met the same fate in the end.

Then, suddenly, catastrophe struck. The Germans' plans entered a new phase of accelerated momentum. In July a senior Gestapo official arrived in Brussels, armed with a set of threatening instructions: the deportation of ten thousand Jews from Belgium had to be expedited without delay. This came in the wake of consultations between the Nazi authorities where the detailed practicalities of carrying out such an enterprise had been thoroughly worked out. The German military administration requested exemption for Jews who had the advantage of Belgian citizenship. It also pointed out that it lacked the means to guarantee the perfect execution of these orders: "the strength of our police force is insufficient for coercive measures", observed one official German report. It was essential that the wretched cohorts of deportees should submit passively to the murderous assault being inflicted upon them. This was where the intervention of the AJB became decisive. Its actions effectively ensured that the deportation of the first contingents took place on what was to all intents and purposes a voluntary basis. The Germans were spared from having to use direct force. The AJB made its own staff available and rounded up the victims, either by giving reassurances to allay anxieties or by issuing threats. This all took the form of a notification which my brother and I received on 31 July 1942.

What happened was this: on that morning around 11 o'clock an official from the *Judenrat* rang our doorbell and handed us a circular for which we were to give him proof of receipt. The circular was headed: "ORDER FOR WORK DUTIES". It came from the military command for Belgium and the north of France and it stipulated that those to whom it was addressed had to present themselves within twelve hours at the Dossin barracks in Malines, which was to be the assembly point for future deportees. The little town of Malines was an ideal location since it was halfway between Brussels and Antwerp, the two main population centres for Jews in Belgium. The circular ordered the victims to bring "provisions for two weeks", as well as "work" clothes and certain items of practical use. It stated clearly that it was "strictly prohibited to make any complaint either to the authorities or to any German or Belgian individuals" and concluded with the warning that "failure to appear at the Reception Centre within the stipulated time will lead to your arrest and deportation to a concentration camp in Germany".

Another communication followed on 1 August, this time written by the AJB itself. In this it was stated that "according to the assurances given by the Occupying Authority, these are in fact work duties and not deportation measures".[8] Also that: "the alarming events of recent days compel us to draw your attention to the fact that disregarding the order for work duties could entail regrettable consequences both for members of your family and for the whole of the country's Jewish population".

So my brother Henri and I had twelve hours to present ourselves at the barracks in Malines. After we had got over the delivery of the circular and our first surprised reactions, we gathered our clothes together and packed our suitcases. On that day, my father was completely absorbed in a project to which he had only referred in the most mysterious terms, and he wasn't at home. Left to our own devices, we decided, with our mother's agreement, that we had no alternative but to

---

8 This assurance was a lie and was known to be so at the *Judenrat*. Under the date 18 July, the journal of one of its principal leaders notes: "It is increasingly confirmed that mass *deportations* of Jews are to be feared."

respond to the notification. I have a clear recollection of those feverish few hours. There was an element of dread and a kind of pride in the excitement we felt. Yes, pride! And I'm sure my memory does not deceive me on this point. When my brother and I paid a visit to some friends that afternoon to say goodbye to them, we quite openly and without inhibition displayed an air of resolve, a martial demeanour, as if we were obeying a call-up order that turned us into soldiers fighting for a noble cause. I can picture myself walking along the street next to Henri, at a marching pace, admiring my brother's calmness and determined to emulate him by remaining steadfast in the face of the test to come.

We did remain steadfast. But when my father got home, he made the decision for us that there would be no test and that we were not to go to Malines. We protested – I remember it still: our refusal to obey would entail reprisals; we were prepared to work hard; we were neither cowards (!) nor deserters (!). My father swept all these protests aside with a categorical reply. He was in no mood to argue and disinclined to use persuasion. He had his mind on other things. He had just taken a bold step, had planned and organised an initiative of the utmost importance; he was about to embark upon an action from which he expected well-nigh miraculous results and these would nullify the circular we had received that morning and all others like it. He had an appointment with Queen Elisabeth, the Queen Mother of Belgium.

The fact was that for days on end the tension had been mounting in Brussels; days when my father had witnessed a few of the dramas unfolding in hundreds of thousands of families. These were erupting in powerless protest, in screams of despair, which for my part I heard only as faint echoes. But my father was at the very centre of the tragedy, at the *Judenrat* headquarters on the Quai du Commerce, where he went every day. Was this because he was still hoping to join it and "make sure the Germans don't get away with anything"? Or because he had a friend there, taken on as one of its middle-ranking officials like numerous workers from Jewish institutions, and that he took advantage of this connection to keep himself informed? Whatever the case, he made daily visits to it and came home distressed. He described the most heartrending scenes: mothers whose children had been summoned to Malines and who were asking for some reassurance about what would happen to them; others with a son or daughter already there and no news of them; men and women pleading with the AJB leaders to grant them an exemption because their departure for the Reception Centre would mean abandoning young children. There was an indescribable mêlée where these weeping parents mingled with the AJB messengers returning or leaving with their fatal notifications. Worst of all, said my father, above the commotion, even more ghastly than the parents' terror, the tears of the mothers and the howling of the children (for some were there too) was the intransigence of the AJB leaders, their harshness, their arrogance and *hauteur*. There was one in particular who stood out because of his cruelty and viciousness. When one poor Jewish woman spoke to him in extremely shaky French that was barely audible or comprehensible, he snapped back with all the superiority of his Belgian citizenship: "Well, well! If you ended up in Eastern Europe what would be wrong with that? You are all from Poland anyway! You'd just be going back where you came from!"

This bourgeois Jew's xenophobia towards recent Jewish immigrants of plebeian extraction was neither exceptional nor specific to Belgium. Writing about attitudes in the German Jewish communities in the years following the Nazi rise to power, no less an able and judicious observer than Alfred Grosser noted that "one section of German Jewry believed that the anti-Semitism of the National Socialists would only be directed at Jews from the lower orders and that Israelites of some standing had nothing to fear so long as they didn't make a fuss." And the historian illustrates this class reflex by quoting the statement of the general secretary of the

The Dossin Barracks at Malines.

Union of Jews of German Nationality:[9] "It was sentimental weakness when the German Jews failed to make up their minds to act against the Jews from the East with the severity that was plainly the duty of every German."[10]

If this severity towards the "Jews from the East" was a duty, it was one carried out with unfailing zeal by the Brussels AJB leader.

We also had reports of the scenes taking place at the camp in Malines. The stripping of the internees, their utter helplessness, the lack of food, the thirst – in that glorious summer of 1942 – the distress of separated families, and the accumulation of all this awfulness further increased the panic of Jews who received notifications from the AJB. Over and over, we had visits from friends telling us about this calamity which worsened almost by the hour. My father said nothing. What he had seen was no

---

9   The German nationals were on the side of the traditional German right.

10   Alfred Grosser, *Dix leçons sur le nazisme*, Paris, 1976, p. 88.

less tragic than what he was hearing now. Then, one evening, as we ate our meal in silence (for once!), he spoke up: "Something has to be done! We must act! We must prevent this catastrophe!"

The next day, he visited all and sundry. He had been to see one of his friends, the president of an important veterans association, and through him met the director of an organisation connected with the Belgian Red Cross. He put him in the picture. They had talked about aid for the Malines internees, but neither of them felt it was enough. So other ideas had come up. They had to aim higher, take the issue much further. And my father had said: "I want to see Queen Elisabeth. She's the only one who can get us out of this!"

At the same time, and even before this, there were Jews who had realised that the catastrophe being prepared and now taking shape called for a response adequate to the danger; that anti-Semitic persecution in its most criminal forms made it absolutely necessary to carry out concerted and clandestine resistance actions of some kind. In other words, a political initiative. What they had in mind was fighting on a variety of fronts, so that the struggle against the Germans would mean both attacking them directly as well as rescuing the men, women and children whom they wished to prey upon and destroy. Such reactions were a matter of temperament, social and ideological ties, and mental attitudes. My father was not resigned to passivity, but he was a patriotic traditionalist and he had deeply embedded beliefs and reflexes regarding authority (he had even named his fourth child after Albert I, the "gallant king"). He was imbued with a blanket ideology of paternalism, faith in philanthropy and respect for people of importance, so for him at this moment of the utmost danger and the utmost distress, it was not in active resistance that help was to be found, but in the benevolent intervention of Queen Elisabeth.

The wife of the most popular and renowned sovereign in the history of the Belgian monarchy was a strange figure. She had shared in King

Albert's triumph for the victories of 1918 and in addition to these laurels she had other, less expected qualities. She was known to be an artist and somewhat unconventional; she was close to Albert Einstein. Later, when the Second World War was over, her interest in the arts would lead to her involvement as organiser of major international music festivals. To the outrage of the deeply anti-communist Belgian establishment and the court, her lack of conformity would draw her sympathies towards Soviet Russia and the People's Republic of China – an outrage all the greater because it was her duty to be discreet. But back in the summer of 1942, Elisabeth of Belgium was preoccupied not with Lenin or Mao, but with saving the Jews of her country.

On 31 July, my father had been informed that the next day he could meet with the Queen at the royal palace in Brussels. But, higher up, it had been deemed judicious for him to be accompanied by official figures from the Jewish world, to give greater weight to his initiative and increase the chances of its success. My father immediately went in search of these individuals. His choice finally settled on two AJB leaders, Eugène Hellendael and in particular S.V., who was at the top of the hierarchy. The interview, which my father often recounted in days to come, took place on the afternoon of Saturday 1 August. The Queen Mother had said little, merely expressing her appalled reactions with an interjection or a word here and there. My father gave her a straightforward, and thus very upsetting, account of what was happening to the Jews. And the Queen Mother promised to "do something", pronouncing that the visit would have an outcome. I shall return to this outcome. For now, I shall confine myself to a report of this event in terms of details which are less insignificant than might at first seem.

As I said, my father was accompanied by two Jewish personalities one of whom in particular, S.V., played a major role in the AJB from its foundation to its dissolution in August 1944, on the Liberation of Belgium. We had known about my father's surprise since his first meeting with this man, a rich furniture manufacturer, whose composure struck him as verging on numbness. When everyone else was in a state, he was icily calm, but in my father's view this impassivity was more a matter of indifference than clear-headedness. After the delegation had been shown into one of the drawing-rooms at the palace in Brussels, they had had to wait for the Queen Mother to arrive. Hellendael and my father had both been very nervous and were having difficulty preparing what they would say to the Queen Mother, so as to find the right words to move her to their cause. S.V. did not involve himself in these anxious preliminaries. He walked around the royal drawing-room quite at his ease, apparently pleased with himself for being there, admiring the furniture and the carpets, picking up objects and studying the pictures, unable to contain his excitement at seeing all these wonderful things. Throughout the interview with Queen Elisabeth he remained silent, and there is every reason to believe that if 1 August 1942 remained a memorable date for him it was more to do with the attractions of the royal furnishings than with the seriousness of the business enacted there. Is this idle speculation? I think not. S.V., a leading light in the AJB, a witness to genocide, and one of its agents, throughout those terrible years kept a wartime journal that constitutes a most improbable and damning piece of evidence, the self-indictment of a prominent Jew:

4 September 1942
[On what he called the "stupid" attacks on the Germans:] The perpetrators lack the courage to give themselves up, and innocent people are paying for the damage.

12 December 1942
[After the Germans had released a Jew married to a non-Jewish woman:] I find it extraordinary that someone should be recompensed for having been unfaithful to his religion.

15 February 1943

We are eating well and I have mentioned that I only want to eat good white bread from now on, for the following reason: if we are going to be taken away, then we should eat well for as long as possible; if we aren't going to be taken then it's business as usual.

31 May 1943

I am very pleased that I can live extremely comfortably.

14 August 1943

The stock exchange is up a little.

11 November 1943

We hear that instructions have come from Berlin to clamp down on the Jewish problem. It seems to be just a matter of mixed marriages.[11] In one sense that would be quite fair.

18 November 1943

Business is picking up a little … It is to be hoped that I'll be able to keep doing well until the war is over, with nothing to hinder me in my work.

23 January 1944

Birthday dinner at L's …: lobster, an utterly delicious bouchée à la reine, fillet steak, potatoes with baby peas, Chester cheese, ice cream, mocha gâteau, coffee, liqueurs, various wines and champagne.

8 February 1944

I'm going to the concert with A … to hear Beethoven's sonatas.

11   Couples in which only one partner is Jewish.

23 March 1944
Business is in the doldrums.

8 May 1944
Business is in the doldrums.

24 June 1944
There are still a lot of roundups in Brussels.

4 July 1944
Business is very slow.

7 July 1944
They're arresting any Jews left in Liège.

22 July 1944
Some small improvement in business, but not much.

1 August 1944
A Jewish transport left yesterday (about 550 people).

Queue for bread at the Boulangerie Louagie, rue de Stalle, Uccle. (Photograph by J. d'Osta.)

25 August 1944

We've won ourselves four years in which nothing dramatic has happened to us, except for my spell in Breendonck,[12] but apart from that we have always stayed in our own apartment, with heating in the winter. Every day we've eaten our fill of meat, butter, eggs and very often cakes; almost always the bread has been practically 100 per cent white.

31 August 1944 [the eve of the liberation of Brussels]

Business is picking up again. I can't believe our good fortune in having escaped all the bad luck. ... But we still have to look out and be careful not to trust practically anyone, especially the jealous ones who've had a bad time of it.

15 September 1944 [soon after the Liberation of Belgium]

The Jewish problems that lie ahead are a very hard to resolve, given the disreputable elements who are dealing with the issue at present.

At present! After the Germans had gone ...

25 September 1944

Jewish affairs have gone awry, because foreign elements have set out to monopolise all the power and they have marginalised the former leaders of the Association. However, the government is going to see to it that Belgians are given the job of taking care of everything, for we've had enough of all the foreigners here sounding so high and mighty and we're going to put them in their place.

Does it need to be spelled out that these "foreigners" who are so high and mighty and have to be put in their place are the Jewish survivors of the genocide?

---

12 In September 1942, some of the *Judenrat* leaders were sent, probably as an intimidatory measure, to the Breendonck concentration camp in Belgium. They stayed there for about a week, then were released.

It isn't only the Jewish outsiders who worry S.V.

28 November 1944
Today, we have the pleasure of a tram strike. ... It's the poor, stirred up by fifth-column agitators, who make the greatest demands.

And, by way of leave-taking (7 May 1945) and concluding his wartime journal:

The drama is over, the curtain has fallen. God be praised, we have got through this sorry period without too much misfortune. Let us try to be just as happy in the new peace.

Just as happy ... He was and remained so. When S.V. died ten or fifteen years later, he was still one of the most prominent leaders of the Jewish community in Brussels.

Meanwhile, however, the drama was still at its height. We did not go to Malines, either on 31 July or 1 August 1942. And shortly after this we received the first signs of the outcome of the visit to Queen Elisabeth by my father and his companions. The director of the Red Cross received a communication from her secretary, and this was passed on to my father. It indicated that the Queen had contacted her daughter, Princess Marie-José, the daughter-in-law of King Victor Emmanuel of Italy, and that the Princess had in turn been in touch with Hitler. The Führer had promised Marie-José of Italy that improvements would be made in the situation of the Jews in Belgium: all of the measures affecting them would be applied in a "humanitarian" manner; in particular, families would not be separated (and indeed, whenever this could be achieved, they ended up together in the gas chambers). Moreover, Jews of Belgian nationality would have nothing to worry about (they were not deported until September 1943). And the Queen added that she would continue to keep an eye on the problem. My father's conclusion was that this was a great victory and that we would win others. This was false: none of the concessions granted by Hitler contradicted the plans made from the outset.

I later learned that the approach made to Queen Elisabeth had been badly received by the Jewish Resistance, who had deemed it to be futile and even dangerous insofar as it confirmed divisions between Belgian and non-Belgian Jews, which is to say well-to-do Jews who would benefit from a reprieve, and poorer Jews from elsewhere. I also learned that Hellendael, who was in touch with members of the Resistance, had been advised not to participate in the delegation, and had, however, taken no notice. It proved fatal to him, since the Gestapo, much irritated by the Queen Mother's intervention, had resolved to take revenge. Although he was protected at the time by his status as a Belgian citizen and, like all the other AJB leaders, had the advantage of a safe conduct, Hellendael was arrested and deported with his whole family. They all died in the camps. As for the Queen Mother herself, she did indeed continue to take an interest in the plight of the Jews. Her appeals and approaches had a bearing on the lives of some Jewish children brought to safety by various Belgian individuals and institutions.

Meanwhile, however, the Germans' huge machinery of destruction continued to grind on.

V

IN THAT AUGUST of 1942, the machinery was harder at work than at any other point in the course of the war. The AJB went on sending out its notifications, thousands of Jews went on responding to them, and the first transports heading for the extermination camps left Belgium. However, there were more and more signs of reluctance. There were probably many like my brother and me who did not go to Malines, and despite the threats made to refractory elements by the *Judenrat*, no one suffered any further harassment. Around the end of August, the flow of "voluntary" arrivals dried up and the Germans decided to strike another blow. At the beginning of September, they moved directly into action: sealing off the Jewish districts of Brussels around the Midi station and, in particular, those parts of Antwerp with the highest concentrations of Jews, they carried out large-scale roundups in which they arrested thousands of people.

My family lived outside the districts targeted and escaped this calamity. But we knew that the threat had escalated and with it the horror which we had imagined to have reached its peak. Accounts reached us describing both the conditions in which the arrests had taken place and what was also happening in the course of the deportations.

We were told about the terrifying scenes that had occurred during the nightly roundups. I have a particular recollection of what a woman friend of my parents told us once when we were having our afternoon snack.

As she spoke, I felt increasingly unwell at first, and then I experienced a real sense of terror. Could anything be more astounding: the description of despairing parents and panicking children as they were woken up in the middle of the night with spotlights, the shouts of soldiers and gendarmes, the sound of boots kicking in doors that stubbornly refused to open. The neighbourhood echoed to the screams of Jews pulled out of their beds, dazed and manhandled. They had a few minutes to throw some clothes into a suitcase before being piled into trucks that took them away to Malines. Sometimes mothers would leave a young child hidden inside a piece of furniture or somewhere out of sight and non-Jewish neighbours would hear the child's cries after the Nazis had left. We heard that in Antwerp the roundups were organised by the Germans with the assistance of the local Belgian police, who had been made available to the occupiers by the city's *bourgmestre*, a prominent figure in the Catholic party. This collaboration was, however, halted after the intervention of Cardinal Van Roey, the Primate of Belgium. As opposed to what happened in France, where the police and the national gendarmerie took it upon themselves to arrest tens of thousands of Jews, in Belgium the action of the Antwerp police was a single "blunder" never to be repeated.

That same day we were also regaled with a detailed account of the first deportations. We were told how dozens of people were crammed together into cattle wagons, without any light or water, often unable to hold back their cries and their tears. We were hypnotised by what our parents' friend told us; we stopped asking her questions and when she had gone we remained as if petrified. I remember that I had a ghastly nightmare that night, and my father tried to calm me down by sprinkling water on me and slapping my face.

Nightmares happened from one moment to the next at that time. One Saturday early in August, for example, there was a panic in the little synagogue at the Rue des Coteaux when prayers had been abruptly disturbed by a muffled sound and a commotion whose significance we didn't

immediately grasp. The noise suddenly became louder and more recognis-
able: German police cars were in the area. We were terribly threatened: the
Gestapo were probably about to burst into the synagogue. Within seconds
the faithful were on their feet, jostling one another in their rush towards
the door. My father, my brothers and I tried not to give in to our fear at
first. It was a matter of dignity! I clung to my seat, feeling a mixture of
self-satisfaction and scorn for all those who lacked our courage and presence of mind. But these noble sentiments fizzled out and we were soon in
the street, pride and family name forgotten as we fled from the synagogue,
thereafter a trap which for a very long time would remain deserted.

Around the same time, I was stopped once in the Rue de la Poste by
an old woman who, in her working-class Bruxellois speech, reminded
me that danger was all around. "Don't go that way, *menneke*, they're
arresting Jews like you in that street."

"But which way should I go?" I asked.

"Come into my house. You won't have to stay long."

Half an hour later, her son was sent out on a recce. The coast was
clear and I could go home.

My elder brother had a more nerve-racking adventure when one day,
by grim coincidence, he had to go to Malines, where my father knew an
obliging miller who now and then was prepared to let us have a few kilos
of flour. Henri collected these supplies, and had set out for the station
when he got the impression that he was being followed. He tried to shake
off the man who had aroused his suspicions, but to no avail. He quick-
ened his step and turned into a maze of narrow streets, yet still failed to
lose his pursuer. In desperation and scared to death, he went into a shop
and told the proprietor that he was in great danger of being arrested.
The shopkeeper took pity on him and led him to the back of the shop,
all the way through the house and garden and into another street. This
gave him the time to run to the station and throw himself on to a train.
He came home to us *that* day, shaking with fright.

— —

It was not just people's reluctance to respond to the *Judenrat*'s notifications any more that prompted the Germans to resort to more terroristic measures for arresting Jews. Something else had happened that played an equal part in this: the intervention of the Resistance, whose actions filled us with enthusiasm and, at one point, with apprehension.

One day in late August my father came home in a state of great agitation. He had just witnessed a rather unusual scene at the AJB headquarters. During a late-afternoon lull in the comings and goings, the doors had been flung open and Germans burst into the main hall where so many heartrending scenes had taken place. Among the jackbooted Nazis was Dr Asche, the chief of the Brussels Gestapo. At once, the AJB leaders came running and my father was dumbfounded to see them stand to attention before the German police. Asche made a thundering speech, from which the following passage stands out in my memory.

"My friend Holzinger has just been murdered, a man of boundless dedication. I warn you that if his murderers are not handed over or have not been found within twenty-four hours, I shall make sure that everything you have experienced so far will seem like child's play." And, singling out the president of the AJB for his next remarks, he barked: "Have I made myself clear, Monsieur Chief Rabbi?"

The Chief Rabbi clicked his heels and answered with laconic submission: "Perfectly, Herr Doktor."

"Do you realise, he clicked his heels for the Gestapo chief!" my father added.

Who was this Holzinger who seemed so precious to the Gestapo chief, now that he had died? He was an AJB functionary who had just been appointed director of the Department for Jewish Work Duties, the man primarily responsible for everyday liaison with the Nazi police. Was his execution an act of justice or intimidation? Or was its aim also to disrupt the deportation services? A month earlier, the Resistance had carried out another action of equal audacity, raiding the *Judenrat* offices and burning the huge set of files containing the names and addresses of tens of thousands of Jews.

When Holzinger died, there was consternation and anxiety in the AJB's governing committee. Homage was paid with all solemnity to his living achievements and it was decided to erect a memorial honouring his memory. The friend of my father's who had a clerical job there, a Jew from Prague, told us that the Association's leaders were in a state of total turmoil at the time. They blamed the assassination on either "German provocateurs" or "bandits".

At any rate, Holzinger's execution did not provoke any serious reprisals from the Germans. Only a few AJB leaders were given any trouble. They were imprisoned for a week or two at the Breendonck concentration camp, not far from Brussels. They were then released and allowed to resume their previous activities.

Recently, I happened to come across two people who had given shelter to the "bandit". The latter was an armed partisan and, like them, a member of the communist resistance networks. A few hours after the execution, he had rung at their door and, no sooner inside, had collapsed into an armchair. He had asked for water and swallowed glass after glass. He was sweating copiously and it was a while before he was able to speak. When he had calmed down, he told them that he had just carried out an "action", without giving any further details. He told them his weapon was jammed and showed them a revolver; this spoke for itself. He had made his getaway on a bicycle, but had been seen by another cyclist who set out in furious pursuit and finally caught up with him. When this man asked why he had acted as he did, the partisan's convincing explanation made the man promise to tell no one what had happened.

Some time later, when he thought he could allow himself to speak more freely, the partisan told his friends why he had been so distraught and emotional as to give himself away that day. "You have no idea what it's like to kill someone for the very first time. It's awful, truly awful!"

Was it even more awful for this Jewish partisan because the man he had to shoot down happened also to be a Jew? This was the kind of extreme measure that the Jewish Resistance sometimes had to decide upon. However, in some instances this posed no problems of conscience. As, undoubtedly, in the case when repeated attempts were made to kill an individual who had acquired a particularly gruesome reputation in the course of the persecutions. "Big Jacques" was a Jew who, for quite unfathomable reasons, had offered his services to the Gestapo and had distinguished himself with tragically effective criminal zeal. This man, whose real name was Icek Glocowsky, drove around Brussels in a black limousine looking for Jews on the streets and bringing about their immediate arrest. He was a legendary figure of sorts, arousing in everyone a profound sense of dread and even stronger feelings of quite unspeakable loathing. "Big Jacques" alone seems to have been responsible for the deportation of some hundreds of Jews.

A number of times, the Resistance tried to liquidate him, but each of these attempts failed because he was so well protected. In June 1944, it was decided to launch an all-out attack. Ten partisans, of whom only two were Jewish, took part in this action, but yet again the outcome was failure and three of them were left behind. With the Liberation, "Big Jacques" disappeared and it was rumoured that the Germans themselves had made it their business to execute him. In March 1947, a Belgian court sentenced him to death in his absence.

His was an extreme and exceptional case of treachery, but this did not make it unique. There were other, more common examples of betrayal, as in the case of those who entered into economic collaboration with the Germans. Foremost among them were the manufacturers of the fur jackets that were delivered in large quantities to German soldiers on the eastern front. Thus, in occupied Belgium there were several sweatshops where some hundreds of Jews earned a paltry income and a precarious degree of protection. For the vast majority of them it was a painfully conscience-racking situation. We knew one of these *vestelmacher* (jacket-makers) since he was engaged to a cousin of my father's. He was ashamed of the occupation into which he had been forced by poverty and insecurity. I am still acquainted with the widow of one of these fur workers (a sector in which Jewish labour had always been very active) and she has talked about how her husband resigned himself to taking on work in one of these sweatshops. The couple and their young child were living in an appalling state of destitution and the wife had begged him to accept this kind of work, but he considered it so ignominious that he kept on refusing until the day when she threatened to kill herself unless he agreed.

But for these hundreds of small craftsmen and workers now reduced to starvation wages (it was deliberately prescribed that their remuneration should be lower than what "Aryans" were paid) there were several dozen Jewish bosses who made a lot of money out of what for them was a very lucrative business. A number of them survived the war, but sometimes the Resistance made them pay with their lives for their doubly scandalous collaborationism.

Then there was the sorry tale of one of my brother Henri's classmates, the son of an extremely wealthy businessman. When the war began we lost touch with him, but in the circumstances it appeared that Monsieur W.'s affairs had not greatly suffered. On the contrary, they prospered so well that some Jewish partisans approached him, asking for financial assistance: 200,000 francs in all. They got a cool reception on their first visit, though Monsieur W. was careful not to refuse since the partisans made sure to place a revolver on the "negotiation table", leaving no doubt about what they were prepared to do. The businessman therefore agreed to pay the hefty sum demanded. He had one cavil, however. "You must realise that I don't have that much money to hand here. Come back in a few days and I'll let you have it then."

Agreement was made to meet a week later. On the day in question, two partisans turned up to see Monsieur W. and encountered a group of Belgian police who had been alerted by the multimillionaire. There was a scuffle, shots were fired and the Gestapo arrived on the scene. The two partisans were arrested, sentenced to death and shot a few months later. The businessman, however, kept his fortune and saved his life. But shortly after the Liberation, he was arrested by former members of the Resistance and interned in the premises they occupied on the Rue de la Source. Monsieur W. was found a few days later, lying mangled on the pavement after a fatal fall from several floors above. The likely truth is that he had been "suicided".

The destruction of the register of Jews that had been drawn up by the functionaries of the *Judenrat*, and the replacement of "voluntary deportation", with "forced deportation" in a sense marked the closing of a period. The roundups of September 1942 ended the most spectacular and most intense days of the persecution. In a matter of weeks, some 13 million Jews had been arrested and transported to the death camps. The great majority of these victims had responded to the notifications of the German authorities and the AJB. Thereafter, it would take the Nazis two years to get their hands on an equal number of Jews. The survivors of the first strikes against the Jewish population were forced to retreat into hiding, an ordeal on the material, physical and mental level which would turn their lives inside out until the country's Liberation, reducing them to a twilight state in which a terror-stricken passivity fed upon constant imaginings or whatever scraps of news got through from the outside world. There was now a substantial risk of being reported by a malicious or greedy neighbour. Everyone was haunted by this threat. They kept out of sight, scrutinising comings and goings, listening for the faintest warning sounds from the street, mentally devising hiding places and emergency escape routes which in the event of a Gestapo raid would almost always prove impracticable. This dread was permanent and contagious. It afflicted Jews and also those who took them in. It was permanent, contagious and lasting. I have never moved into a house or an apartment without instinctively wondering whether it would have been possible to make my escape from it at a moment of danger during a war.

At this stage, the implacable lottery of means once again played havoc. It had operated in May 1940, when for the most part only the wealthiest had been able to flee from continental Europe and take refuge in Britain and the United States. Later, those who could afford to pay for the services of a *passeur* to get them across the frontier, headed for Switzerland. And for those left in Belgium, the constraints of life in hiding also necessitated ever greater expenses. The more affluent had got themselves exemption cards from the AJB, for which they paid very steep prices. There were also Jews who were released from the Dossin barracks in Malines in exchange for a "ransom" which might be as high as one million francs (at 1940s values) or even higher. The shared condition of Jews intended for collective extinction did not therefore prevent social differences from further shaping the fates of the oppressed. If being Jewish was then the worst of misfortunes, the plight of poor Jews brought them even closer to total impotence and utter doom.

There was, however, one exception to this rule of obeisance to the distinctions of money and class, a very striking and very edifying exception which I only found out about later. It applied to the Jews of Charleroi, the big industrial centre in the south of Belgium. This Jewish community had some quite distinctive features. There were practically no Belgian nationals and the level of income was relatively low. The Jews of Charleroi included plenty of small shopkeepers and craftsmen, but no representatives of what we might call the bourgeoisie, while on the other hand there was a substantial proletarian contingent, which went some way to explaining the links between these Jews and the Belgian socialist and communist organisations in the region, as well as their connections to the trade union movement.

It was militants of the far left who, at the very start of the Occupation, decided to unite and plan for resistance with the formation of Jewish Solidarity in Charleroi (*Solidarité Juive de Charleroi*). When the persecutions began in the summer of 1942, they were better prepared than those elsewhere and not so defenceless. The experience of working outside the law protected them from any illusions that could have been fostered by a "policy of pursuing the lesser evil" of the kind upheld by the AJB. The reality of being rooted in national and local political life made their situation and their outlook very different from those of Jews in Antwerp or Brussels.

Indeed, every time the occupier went on the offensive, the Jewish resistance group in Charleroi convened to come up with an effective response. In May 1942, when the deportations to the north of France began, a number of Jews moved to Charleroi, where they thought they would be less exposed than in the major Jewish centres. The Solidarity militants sometimes managed to find these "refugees" jobs as factory workers. Two months later, they set themselves the task of thwarting the German plan which used the AJB as mediator in the "voluntary" process of rounding up deportees at Malines. They visited many of the families affected by the notifications and urged them not to respond. They were often successful. But it was in late September 1942 that they revealed a measure of daring and resourcefulness that was to stymie the Nazis' progress.

On 23 September, the occupying authorities demanded that the AJB in Charleroi hand over the complete and up-to-date list of Jews living in the region. But this local branch of the *Judenrat* differed fundamentally from the Antwerp and Brussels branches, and from the AJB's national governing body. The Charleroi Jews, or more precisely their political centre, asked one of the few prominent Jews in the city to represent their community on the AJB. This delegate was there to put out feelers and report back on how the situation was developing. When, on the evening of 23 September, he received from the Germans the order to provide them with the list of the city's Jewish inhabitants, he gathered his comrades together and they all set about considering how to block this move.

The stratagem was found: throughout the night, a team drew up a bogus list on which the real names of the Jews were matched to imaginary addresses which the team had been careful to locate around the outskirts of the city in order to disperse the Nazis as they set out to search the different premises. It was this bogus list that the Charleroi president of the AJB gave to the city's Kommandatur on 25 September. Virtually at the same time, in the early hours, groups of militants travelled all over the city to warn Jews that the Germans would attempt to arrest them that very day. They urged those who were still living at their registered address to move out at once. Their flight was facilitated by the collaboration between Jewish Solidarity and their "Aryan" political and trade union comrades. It was this joint enterprise that enabled a large number of hiding places to be organised where Jews could find refuge.

The ruse worked. The Nazis were sent on a wild goose chase, which lost them precious time and was turned to good account to deprive them of hundreds of their prey. More than anywhere else, solidarity between Jews and non-Jews on the left, the goal of Jewish Solidarity ever since its inception, was to play a salutary role. But this happy outcome was achieved only because lengthy preparations had been carried out, because favourable circumstances had made it possible to overcome the isolation of the Jewish population, and ultimately because individuals strengthened by a keen political awareness, then toughened by militancy and clandestine actions, had set up a barrier to German aggression. In this working-class Belgian city, a grain of sand – tiny, but hard and indissoluble – had checked the Nazi machine.

VI

IN 1942, HISTORY was at odds with meteorology. With the start of autumn, after the summer's great shocks, our long hibernation began.

The period of large-scale departures for Malines was over; the roundups in the Jewish districts had run their course; the arrests had assumed more insidious forms; the figures for the deportations had dropped sharply and we had begun to hope that, with a few precautions, we might survive the slaughter. But in my family, whether through thoughtlessness or helplessness, precautions were quite minimal.

In most instances, surviving Jews had left their registered address and gone underground. The case of the Parisian relative whom I have already mentioned is perhaps in this respect an extreme one, but it is significant: he, his father and his younger brother had hidden themselves away in a tiny, cramped workshop space, and there they were joined by seven other people. Throughout the two years between the start of the major persecutions and the Liberation, the adults never ever left their hiding place, not for a single hour, and it was the two children who ensured that food was found for this small community forced into idleness, a prey to boredom, fear, despair, jealousy and hatred.

We too came to know idleness and boredom, but we resolved not to cut ourselves off from the outside world. We were well aware that there were other Jews who no longer took the risk of being out there. We refused to follow their example completely, even though we reduced our sorties outside. As ever, this "dignified" response was part and parcel of the family atmosphere fostered by my father. His determination to put on a brave face, without ever undertaking any genuinely courageous action, derived from a quixotic posture full of weakness. So we went out now and then, sometimes because we needed to, and sometimes out of bravado.

Real clandestinity would have required false papers as well as caution. These were obtained by the wealthy and by Resistance activists, but we were neither and this aggravated the precariousness of our situation. And its discomfort increased the longer our plight lasted. We were still living in the spacious bourgeois house that we had occupied since 1939, but by some symbolic coincidence, the house underwent a change in the autumn of 1942. It became more cramped, as if the walls were closing in on us. Our landlord was carrying out alterations which meant that one or other part of the house, one floor after another, became uninhabitable. This was very inconvenient at a time when we found ourselves stuck at home, our imprisonment scarcely alleviated by our intermittent outings.

We had to be organised in every single respect. We had to provide ourselves with food, which involved not just shopping, but also getting hold of the ration cards given out by the municipal administration. There were, however, rumours that the Germans were keeping a close watch on the centres where the cards were distributed. Some Jews could afford to acquire the services of a neighbour; others, the wealthiest, gave up their meagre official rations and used only the black market – all of which was well beyond our means. This meant that we had to present ourselves at the municipal offices, where my brother and I took turns. And since we had perforce to carry out these procedures, my father did some of his friends a favour by having us undertake these dangerous tasks on their behalf too, acts of charity that would ultimately prove fatal.

All the same, poverty made our hunger all the more nagging and severe. At one point my father thought he was going to get a well-paid job that would have alleviated our financial hardship. In Brussels, during the summer of 1939, we had made the acquaintance of a Polish Jew who had only recently arrived in the country and was in a state of total destitution. My father had helped him to put his official situation in order and then had lost touch with him. In the winter of 1943, he had a chance encounter with this man and was impressed by his air of prosperity; it was clear that he had managed to adapt to his new circumstances successfully. He was in splendid form and looked every inch the well-heeled man of substance. And he certainly was well-heeled, having done wonderfully in business. He offered my father the chance of going into partnership with him and made an appointment for them to meet at his business premises. When my father got there he found a warehouse well stocked with every kind of merchandise. He asked the entrepreneur a few questions about the precise nature of the business activity that had made him so wealthy and received only evasive answers. My father thought this must have involved either the black market or supplying to the Germans, but since he deemed both these activities equally odious, he turned down the offer, went back to his high-minded poverty and kept his honour intact. The businessman, for his part, kept on getting richer, maintained a relationship with the Germans which was doubly fruitful since it allowed him both to consolidate and increase his wealth, while at the same time paying handsomely to save Jewish children from falling into the hands of the Germans. Moreover, he bankrolled the AJB with a monthly allowance of 20,000 francs: a small fortune. When the war was over, no honours were spared him.

Organising our "pastimes" was no easy matter either. When school began again in September, though not for us, we made up our minds to go on with our studies somehow. One of my brother Henri's classmates agreed to bring him his notes and exercise books, while Henri did his best to teach us the subjects he himself had been taught the previous year. For a few weeks, we kept this up, but then our enthusiasm waned, it became too much of an effort, and that was the end of that.

How else could we kill the time? My father, no longer able to play bridge, at which he excelled, managed extremely well, for days and months on end, without ever tiring of this idleness, and without ever helping my mother, who was even busier than before, now that she had to do without household help of any kind. As for the boys, we were faithful to our father's example, putting our minds to doing nothing and succeeding perfectly well. Our activities only extended to inventing games whereby we could practise sports indoors and even on paper. Football, cycling and athletics competitions were reduced to a series of moves where the skill lay in using dice instead of a ball, or else stacking playing cards to make an athletics course, and marking out the floor as a mountain path. So the hours passed, and the days, and the months in which tedium bred intimacy. The warmth of our family, in which we took refuge, gave us a semblance of safety. Being forced back on our own resources was an experience that marked us all in one way or another for the rest of our lives, and it heightened that feeling which the course of events would, however, cruelly undermine.

Of course we read too, but our reading was frugally rationed since there was no question of any of us being able to buy books. All we could do was rummage through what the public libraries had to offer, for, in spite of everything, we continued to use these. However, out of administrative zeal, they unvaryingly applied a rule that had made no provision for the situation of Jewish children who were confined indoors and at a loose end, and this imposed ridiculous quotas on our loans. Added to this there were very strict criteria on the sections open only to adults, which were naturally forbidden to us. Once we had devoured our all too few books, we went back to our endless games of imaginary football or symbolic Tour de France, in which there was a certain component of nostalgia alongside the pleasure of play. The football grounds had been closed to us. On the day when my father had allowed us to go to a match the afternoon ended badly: a German officer was watching us closely and when he suddenly started moving towards us, we rushed out of the Anderlecht Stadium in a state of visceral fear before the game was over.

Around the same time my brothers and I went to Marie-Louise Square to a "pelota" match that lasted longer than expected. The minutes went by and our enjoyment was gradually overtaken by fear of our father whom we had failed to inform about the outing. We wanted to leave, but we were stuck in a crowd so thick there was no room to move. My parents were crazy with anxiety as they awaited our return. We were worried about what would greet us at home: would anger get the better of relief? Not caring to take any risks, my brothers sent me on as scout. They had the right idea, for as soon as I stepped into the hallway I was given a resounding slap on the face. This calmed my father's nerves and dampened my passion for outdoor sports. From then on we settled for indoor pastimes.

Usually we went out early in the morning since it was believed that street surveillance was slacker then. But it was rumoured that "big Jacques" had started getting out and about earlier in the day. We had to give up these walks. The kingdom of the night remained. It was more hospitable and, what was something new for children, darkness soothed our fears. My father in particular took advantage of it to visit neighbours and listen to the "British radio". Sometimes, he stayed out for longer than usual; imperceptibly, I would be gripped by a worry that would grow and turn into real fear. I will always remember those anxious times after nightfall. From my bed, I listened out for every sound made in the street and carefully watched the approach of passers-by, who were few and far between. In the end I could recognise my father's rapid stride and I still cannot attempt to describe my growing and halting sense of relief whenever I finally was able to identify his walk and know he was there. I was bathed in an indescribable warmth, experiencing a moment of acute happiness before life resumed its rhythm then dissolved into a sleep of near contentment.

Around the end of November, the house became even more cramped and life became even harder.

In the summer, my grandfather, his wife and my Antwerp uncles, aunts and cousins had left their city and gone into hiding in the countryside, not far from the French border. There, they had found a large house and, with the protection of the rural police and some of the villagers, they thought they were safe.

Then, one evening our doorbell rang, an extremely rare event. My father thought twice about opening the door; we were all drilled only to answer if visitors rang the bell with a double short ring. It rang again. He opened up to find his brother, whom we were very surprised to see since we knew that he had taken refuge along with the others in the village of Tournaisis. A few days earlier, the Germans had burst into the house and arrested my grandfather, his wife and several of their relatives. He himself and four others (an uncle of mine and three cousins) were in an attic at that moment. They kept quiet until these members of their close family had been taken away in the Gestapo cars. They took the precaution of hauling themselves up into the loft and stayed there until the next day. That day, they heard the sound of boots stamping around and thought the Germans had come back. They stayed in their hiding place and, when they heard the same kind of sounds yet again, thought it best not to move. For four days, while they waited for silence to fall over the house, they had nothing to eat but raw potatoes. After that, they made their escape and took refuge with the village police. My uncle had found a "hidey-hole" for himself, but the four other survivors of the tragedy had nowhere else to turn but to us.

They arrived the next day. Among them was my father's brother-in-law, a diamond craftsman and a quiet, self-effacing man, together with his two sons and a distant cousin. Their being with us added greatly to our problems. We felt very sorry for their misfortune, but it had certain compensations. The two young people, Arthur and Maurice, had long been our friends. Maurice was eighteen and had considerable standing in our eyes, because of his age, his intelligence and his already abundant academic achievements. With him and under his supervision, our studies recommenced, this time in earnest and to our greater interest. Arthur, the younger one, for his part brought us joviality and humour.

Happily, their good nature had withstood the hardships and dangers. Arthur had gone through a number of ordeals. He and a friend of his had been entrusted to a *passeur* who, for a hefty sum, had undertaken to smuggle them both into Switzerland. They had travelled through France without any problems, but at Pontarlier they had a brush with the gendarmes. Nonetheless, they had got out of this tight spot in the end and the Swiss border, so long the object of their hopes and fears, was crossed at night.

On their arrival in a small town some twenty or thirty kilometres inside Switzerland, the two refugees were apprehended by the Swiss police. It was clear that their papers were not in order. They stated that they were Jewish and had come from occupied Belgium. This explanation was not deemed adequate, and, although they pleaded with the gendarmes, their pleas went unheeded. They were taken back to the frontier and were immediately expelled back into France. They succeeded in making their way to Belgium again, but, alas, their success was not complete. One of the two, my cousin Arthur, ended his days in Auschwitz, a victim of Nazism and perhaps also of that legendary Swiss hospitality. For though countless refugees found shelter in Switzerland, there were also a great many cases of expulsion. Moreover, what is one to make of this statement, from one of the more recent and more serious studies of Nazism, that around 1938:

> Switzerland made numerous statements and approaches to the Nazi authorities to prevent Jewish refugees from entering its territory. It was at the instigation of the Swiss that not long after this, Jews in the Third Reich had their passports taken away to be replaced by a special identity document bearing the letter J (Jude) in indelible red print over one inch high, a distinctive marker that would make it easier for them drive back these undesirables at their frontiers.[13]

So Maurice and Arthur were with us, sharing our lessons, our games and our meagre fare. Their father seemed to have no resources and could not contribute to the financial upkeep of our small community. There were now ten of us whom my mother had to feed. By increasing her exertions and her ingenuity, but also by sharing out her children's rations, she nonetheless managed to do so without ever complaining. This lasted until Thursday 7 January 1943, at 2.30 in the afternoon.

I can see it all now and I can relive the scene today with total recall. I had just crossed the road on my way back from a neighbour's house and I was hurrying to our door when I saw two men dressed in leather overcoats getting out of a big black car which had stopped a few yards away from our house. I realised at once who they were and I suddenly felt weak, as if I were about to collapse, and I said to myself: "That's it, it's over now!"

It wasn't over, far from it; it was just the start of a nerve-racking game of bluff, whose unexpected progress I watched with initial dumbfoundment. The two Gestapo men, soon joined by a third, told us they had come to arrest us. We started packing. My youngest brother, who was

13 Grosser, *Dix leçons sur le nazisme*, p. 216.

only six, panicked and threw himself into my arms. Then he calmed down and went into the kitchen, opened a cupboard and filled his pockets with macaroni. "We'll need this at Malines," he whispered, turning to me.

His composure was short-lived. A few minutes after that one of the Gestapo men found him under a bed and dragged him out roughly. My brother again came to me for protection. My mother was busy and my brother Henri was out. My father was preoccupied. Since the moment the Germans had burst into the house, he had been watching them very closely, observing their movements and, in particular, paying keen attention to every word they said.

I have already described how my father had in his youth spent a number of years away from home. He had lived for some time in Bavaria and the way the Gestapo men spoke immediately struck him as familiar. He thought he recognised the Bavarian accent and when he answered their questions he deliberately slipped a few Munich turns of speech into his flawless German. Surprised, the Germans asked him where he came from. My father then talked about the little Bavarian towns he had once known. The Nazis thawed. Then they started reminiscing about the good old days. The seduction attempt had succeeded and my father moved on to the second phase of the operation.

He showed them an old AJB card that in July 1942 had given some semblance of protection to its bearers, of whom there had been many, including all the office holders of Jewish welfare organisations deemed to be in the public interest. As the secretary of a friendly society, my father had received one of these *Ausweiss* cards. It had quickly lost its usefulness and my father had often been on the point of throwing it away, but my mother had made him promise not to; for once he had followed her good advice. It was this worthless document that saved us, because it was put to use at the right time.

The German police asked a few questions about the card, since it didn't match any of the current exemption regulations, but they were willing to give the benefit of the doubt to a man who was so well acquainted with Bavaria in the good old days.

"Everything is in order; we won't take you away, not you or your family," one of them told us.

Then they began quizzing everyone about who they were. Since Henri was out, my father tried to pass my cousin Arthur off as his son, but Arthur wasn't having any of this. Because the protection afforded by the AJB *Ausweiss* extended only to the beneficiary's wife and children, my Antwerp relatives were urged to hurry up with their packing. However, when their papers were examined, it turned out that the elder of my two cousins had Belgian nationality, and one of the Nazis then told him that he was free too.

"I don't care," said Maurice. "You arrested my mother a few weeks ago and now you're arresting my father and my brother. I'm going with them."

This response discomfited the Germans. Doubtless for administrative reasons, these police bureaucrats were loath to arrest someone for whom the regulations made no provision for deportation. An argument got under way with the Gestapo men attempting to make an eighteen-year-old Jewish boy appreciate the attractions of freedom and the futility of grand gestures of solidarity. My cousin wouldn't let himself be persuaded and before long he took his place with the others in the Gestapo car and left for Malines, going on from there to Auschwitz. His fate is heavy with meaning. He died as a martyr, choosing death, and this touching choice, which cut down his young life, has a symbolic value. My cousin could have opted for revenge, or more simply, for struggle. The thought that he could spend the rest of the time left to him fighting against those murderers did not occur to him. While the greatness of his sacrifice would make it sacrilegious to blame him here, we can still reflect upon his actions. One may well ask why, at a time when arms were being taken up all over Europe to bring down a murderous enemy, this young man did something that made him doubly a victim. The victim first and foremost of barbarism, but also in certain respects of a condition and a philosophy that turned him and so many others into unarmed and help-less human beings to be sacrificed, into pitiable corpses, and ultimately into an immense throng, a vast charnel house of broken hearts and bod-ies ground to dust; yet when the time came for great uprisings and struggles to the death, not into fighters, not into a resistance.

There was no cowardice in this submission to "fate". Far from it; it took a lot of courage for Maurice to refuse the safety being offered to him. But his stance of poignant passivity reproduced what is so often bred in human beings, though with the additional circumstance of his being Jewish. Through their traditions and religious culture, the Jews preserved a sense of their unhappy condition that remained unchal-lenged across the centuries. They took consolation and refuge in the messianic dream and the exaltation of martyrdom. This response was both profoundly noble and absurdly powerless and it let the murderers have free rein, so that they became the unassailable perpetrators of an inevitable destiny. Maurice had been educated at a Jewish school in Antwerp. Just at the time when he delivered himself into the hands of the Germans, one of the school's religious teachers – perhaps even his teacher – was arrested and incarcerated at Malines. From the Dossin barracks he wrote a letter impregnated, to the very point of non-sense, with a philosophy of abdication and sacrifice:

> Dear and loyal friends, as you can see, for me the words have been fulfilled: "the Almighty has sent me on his way". I am very glad that this has come about … I have said here … "We are happy, for our fate is to be envied". At first sight it is hard to understand … But this is the truth: if a people such as this exists … and thus the Almighty accompanies it, then this means that "we are happy". Why then should we be troubled? I feel great joy, thanks be to God, and I beg you to be at peace … Have

not some of our "great men" taken it upon themselves to go into exile?
Now that this arises for me, I shall not rebel in any way, not in the least.

We found ourselves alone again: distraught, miserable and scared.
When Henri got home, shortly after the departure of the Germans and
their victims, he began to sob, but the rest of us were dry-eyed. Our
tears only came later; they were tears of rage, of sadness, and humilia-
tion too. And it was not only the Nazis who prompted them, but quite as
much and in a very strange way, those members of our family who had
just been torn away from us.

When we started cleaning and tidying the rooms they had occupied I
found under one of the beds a store of provisions that had been carefully
concealed from us. There was bread, cheese, biscuits and I don't know
what else. My uncle and my cousins, whom we had believed to be pen-
niless, had got this food and kept it exclusively for themselves. When we
went to bed at night, always hungrier than before, they would have a
secret feast to top up the meal that was all the more frugal because of
their being with us. We were aghast.

A few minutes later, we were even more appalled when we came across
a thick notebook, the diary of my cousin Maurice. We did not resist the
guilty desire to peruse it, and we paid a heavy price for this indiscretion.
Among these daily jottings were a good many passages about us. Our
family failings were the target for the author's sarcasm and he had sav-
aged his prey with relish. My mother's self-effacement was presented as
evidence of her utter mediocrity. My brothers and I received less attention but nothing was spared us either. But to our greatest astonishment –
for we imagined that he at least was beyond criticism – it was my father
on whom Maurice came down hardest, scathingly noting faults whose
existence we had never even suspected. Every foible, any and every
absurdity in this figure of whom we had always stood in awe, was
exposed to ridicule, possibly exaggerated, and commented upon at length.

(Above) Maurice: A cruel onlooker.
(Below) Author in 1942.

I am not certain whether my father ever came across these pages. I can recall my brothers' shock and my own consternation. My cousin had been nothing more than a cruel onlooker; we saw him as a monster of spitefulness and ingratitude and that night it grieved me that I could not weep for his arrest as a calamity which gave him the right to my tears.

My father's cleverness and clear head had saved us, but we had no safeguard against a second visit from the Gestapo. Wouldn't they realise that they had been gulled as soon as they checked a list of those genuinely under the *Judenrat*'s protection? Moreover, the Gestapo's arrival had probably been the result of someone giving us away, and whoever was responsible for this malicious deed might well act again when they saw we had escaped arrest. A few years after the war had ended, my father was called as a witness at the trial of a Rexiste who turned out to have been the informant. I recognised him right away. He was a neighbour, an imposing and severe-looking man who had worn a black uniform ever since the start of the Occupation, and this had made him hateful in our eyes. We would often meet him when we were playing in the street and we made a point of never saying hello. Nonetheless, it had not crossed our minds that he could be capable of such a vile action. In any case, on that occasion it had come to nothing, since his letter of denunciation had been intercepted by postal workers in the Resistance and had never reached the Gestapo. This was far from being an isolated case: a great deal of the mail sent to the German police was spotted at the central post office in Brussels and confiscated by patriotic workers there. Eventually the Nazis suspected something of the kind and sent letters to themselves as a way of checking, then they put their own men in the post office, which disrupted the Resistance activities. But, for us, when the Gestapo did eventually turn up at our registered address this was an indication of our own foolhardiness. It was time to move.

Or rather, it was time to make a run for it, for everything about our departure had the air of a getaway. Within a few days, my father found an apartment to let in the same street where we were living, the rue de la Consolation, which so ill deserved its name. Our new home was simultaneously very close and very far away. The street ran either side of a very wide avenue lined with trees that, halfway along, virtually partitioned it into two very different sections. The upper part, where we had lived, was an area of bourgeois residences whose occupants were the comfortably off. The lower section consisted of working-class housing, some of it dilapidated premises. This was a different world. There, my father had come across a shabby apartment in a rundown building. For all that, the rent being asked by the owners was high, and they must have realised that we could not afford the luxury of quibbling over their terms. Later, when fresh calamities sent us on the run again, my father continued to pay this inflated rent for the sake of storing our furniture there. On one occasion, my mother found herself wandering the streets of Brussels alone and in search of somewhere to spend the night; thinking she could take refuge in this apartment and sleep in her own bed she went there, only to find strangers in occupancy. They were the landlord's family.

"There's no room for you here," they told her.

"But I don't have anywhere else to go. It's well after curfew."[14]

"All right, you can stay here tonight. But tomorrow morning, you're out!"

The next morning, she left.

So we couldn't be too fussy about where we lived, or about who the landlord was, nor even less about how we moved house. For security reasons, it was impossible for us to hire the services of a removal firm and a handcart did the job. Fortunately, it was only a short distance to the secret apartment (our father did not declare our change of address) from the house we were leaving. Over several evenings we went back and forth many times between the two, praying that these comings and

---

14 Jews had been prohibited from leaving their homes between eight in the evening and eight in the morning.

goings would not attract too much attention from the neighbours or be interrupted by the arrival of a police patrol.

The day came for us to move out. The house was empty. I walked through the deserted rooms and for a few moments I stood quietly by myself in the midst of this desolation. I had the feeling of being wrenched away for ever from the closeness and warmth of the past. It was in this house that I had experienced the happy days before the war; in this house, already peopled with ghosts, that a family had gathered and was now being wiped out. There was the garden, where last year – before the deluge – we had grown plants now dead, never to revive; where we had protected the last of our carefree games against the outside world; where we had warmed ourselves one last time in an autumn sunshine all of our own. And in front of the house, the roadway, the pavement, even the cobblestones were part of our empire: the theatre of our pleasures and entertainments which were now going to be cut short and would be no more.

My father called me. It was time to go. I was the one who closed the door on our past and the peaceful delights of a long-sheltered childhood.

Our new home was never anything like the old one. It was very poor and its seediness seemed a sign of how much we had come down in the world. That at any rate was how I experienced it throughout the endless winter and the deceptive spring that followed our move there. Along with my youngest brother, I had to share my parents' bedroom in a large room that had once been used as a shop. Henri and Léon got a store room that was turned into their sleeping quarters and also served as our workroom and playroom. There was also a yard which could have offered us some distractions; but it was creepy, and, worse still, it was enclosed by the walls of a biscuit factory whose occupants could easily see us and discern on our faces the Semitic features that sealed our fate. The toilets were in the cellar and the bathroom was only a nostalgic memory. My parents kept on telling us that we had nothing to complain about; their arguments struck us as well founded but unpersuasive.

However, there was one room, the dining-room, that served me as a sanctuary. It was sacred to me for two reasons: it was where those few pieces of furniture we possessed had been placed and thus they recalled our erstwhile prosperity; but it had above all the advantage of being in a sense cut off from the outside world. From it I could see neither the hostile street nor the disquieting yard. I spent long intervals in this room, outside time, as if I were somehow summoning the past and plunging straight into it. The war seemed unreal, the danger had vanished, and peace of mind had been recovered.

It was in this room too that we celebrated the Sabbath, which retained its privileges and seductions to the end. Did we feel at the time that the intimacy of this celebration, with its miraculously preserved peacefulness and the sweetness of a commonality that was as yet unbroken, all that warmth imbued with light and music, was the more precious for being threatened, its limits set by such chilling dangers? I can't remember a single Sabbath coming to an end then without me saying: "We have to keep going for a week; just seven days and the enchantment will begin all over again."

This enchantment had its days already numbered.

And in this same room, something else happened, something extremely solemn and profoundly moving.

I've already said that my father had a friend who worked at the AJB in a junior clerical position. His name was Karniol and he was a Czech citizen from a very bourgeois family background. He had a very loving relationship with his wife, a young woman of such refinement that this, even more than what remained of a jealously preserved elegance, betrayed her equally patrician origins.

They had arrived in Belgium just before the war. They lived in a poverty of such dignity that it added to their charm. Things were very hard for Karniol; fortunately, he had only one young child to feed, but as well as the difficulties of everyday life, his job was far from easy. What a way to earn a living! He was an impotent witness to the horrific scenes I have already described, the servant of an institution he detested, the prisoner of a role that shamed him, at the beck and call of superiors whose callousness filled him with hatred.

One of the last anecdotes he told us speaks volumes about the appalling things that were happening then. Jewish parents had gone to the *Judenrat* to demand that their children who were being held there be given back to them. After being boarded out to non-Jews, these children had been arrested by the Gestapo and, for reasons unclear to me, handed over to the AJB to be looked after. The children were there, locked in a room a few feet away from the main hall where their parents were pleading with the Association's leaders. The latter were obdurate: they had a responsibility for the children for which they were answerable to the Germans and they refused to give up this responsibility. However, at one point, a young boy managed to get out of the room where he was confined, found his way into the main hall and, seeing his father there, ran into his arms. The father took advantage of the general hubbub and rushed out into the street, making for the nearest tram stop. One of the senior figures in the *Judenrat* ran after him. He caught up with him and tried to take the little boy away. An argument ensued and a crowd gathered.

"If you don't give me back the child, I'll telephone the Gestapo!" screamed the AJB leader.

Karniol was often present in the course of similar dramas. And then his own turn came. One day in March 1943, his wife was arrested. His job at the *Judenrat* afforded him scant protection, or perhaps this extended no further than himself. His efforts to liberate his wife got nowhere and he decided to give himself up. He placed his child with non-Jewish friends and, one Saturday at noon, came to bid us farewell before taking the train to Malines.

He had lunch with us and, to our great surprise, seemed almost happy. We had a lump in our throats when he first arrived, but his composure spread to us too.

The meal was nearly over and the time for his departure approached. Once again, the tension mounted. Then Karniol, who had had a very un-Jewish childhood and had discovered the ancestral customs and rituals only when he got to know us, took advantage of a pause in the conversation to begin chanting "Vetaër libenou", the chant that belongs both to the Jewish liturgy and folklore. We joined in, our voices strangely steady. I can see him now, rising to his feet just as the canticle finished, going up to each of us and embracing us one by one, full of serenity. With his suitcase in one hand, he waved to us with the other, a big friendly wave. Smiling, he disappeared in search of his wife.

Both of them died in the camps.

VII

IN APRIL 1943, we celebrated Passover. It had a special significance that year. The festival commemorating the enslavement and liberation of the Hebrews in Egypt and the liturgy that went with it acquired a value that was more than symbolic in the early spring of 1943. For the first time, we found that it faithfully echoed the conditions of our experience and also our great longing for freedom.

A few days later we heard that, on the very eve of Passover, the Jewish Resistance had succeeded, in giving fresh meaning to the old epic legends: the 19 April saw the start of the Warsaw ghetto uprising, whose last remnants stood with weapons in hand against whole SS divisions. That same day a partisan action was organised in Belgium to free what was by then the twentieth convoy taking Jewish deportees from Malines to Auschwitz.

This operation was the brainchild of Gert Jospa, a Jewish engineer of Bessarabian origins. He was someone I got to know much later, just when he was leaving the Communist Party after long years of militancy, a cause he had espoused and adhered to ever since the first flush of youth. It was at the time of the public split between the Soviet Union and the People's Republic of China; Jospa would have no truck with "revisionism" and allied himself with the first European Maoists. Even though I had never been a Communist, he confided in me about his misgivings and uncertainties. He impressed me with the enormous breadth of his political knowledge and the strength of his integrity. This was not the first time that Jospa had faced such a situation. He told me how deeply he had been troubled by the revelations of the Soviet Communist Party's 20th Congress in 1956, and that the attempts of Party leaders to smooth things over had never succeeded in reassuring him. Jospa was to die before his time.

Once he had come up with the plan to intercept the trainload of deportees, Gert Jospa went to Jean Terfve, the future Belgian Communist Party leader who was to become a government minister shortly after the Liberation. At the time, Terfve was in charge of the armed partisan groups. He considered the plan foolhardy in the extreme and ill thought out: what would they do with the hundreds of prisoners they hoped to rescue from the Nazis? How were they to scatter them? Who would be responsible for giving them homes? Jospa was not discouraged and made contact with a different resistance organisation, the G Group, but with no better success. However, the idea was not abandoned. It was taken up by a tiny handful of young people and ultimately suffered from being over-improvised. The heroes of this adventure were novices acting on their own initiative. Yura Livchitz and two of his (non-Jewish) classmates from the Uccle[15] Athénée in Brussels, Jean Franklemont and Robert Maistriau, carried out this bold operation by themselves. For a long time, what actually took place remained a mystery and gave rise to the "legend of the twentieth transport". The truth was recently established, thanks to one historian's investigations.

In fact, the action launched by the three partisans combined with another actually planned inside the Dossin barracks at Malines. Over time, the character of the barracks' population had changed. Along with the thousands of unfortunates caught unawares by a terrorism hitherto

15 Uccle is a middle-class district of Brussels (Trans.).

(Above) The inspirational Gert Jospa, centre, a few months after his return from the camps.
(Below) Yura Livchitz.

unsuspected and overtaken by sudden catastrophe, there were prisoners who had been in the transit camp much longer and who sometimes found an opportunity to organise. Among them were former prisoners who had escaped from earlier convoys but had been recaptured by the Germans. There were also partisans who had ended up in the Dossin barracks because they were Jews and who had not resigned themselves to passive acceptance of their fate. By means of various ruses, they had managed to get hold of tools such as hammers, saws and axes, hiding these among their personal effects. As soon as the train got moving, these men set to work, though only after having had to overcome the reluctance of their companions and the outright opposition of those designated by the Germans as the keepers of "order" in the wagons. Once under way, their work made rapid progress and within only a few miles a large number of deportees were jumping out on to the railway line, with German guards shooting at them as they made a run for it.

Nevertheless, the transport still went on its way. Though not for long. Around Wespelaere, outside Leuven, the driver saw a man on the track waving a red lamp. It was Yura Livchitz. The locomotive braked and the transport came to a standstill. Immediately, Franklemont and Maistriau made a dash to open the wagons. Their plan was hindered when it turned out that the German guard was not, as they had thought, at the back of the train, but had, alas, been divided, with the first section at the very front, in a position to intervene and upset the whole operation. All in all, a mere five deportees were freed by the three partisans. But before the train had reached Wespelaere, and even after the operation, a much higher number had managed to escape. The statistics speak for themselves: 1,631 people had been put on board at Malines in the makeshift station the Germans had built right outside the Dossin barracks. Of these, 231 jumped off the moving transport and five were freed when the train was intercepted at Wespelaere. The Germans shot down twenty-six fugitives and arrested around ninety more, either immediately after or in the week that followed. Nonetheless, the combined action of resistance from the outside and from within led to more than 100 prisoners being saved. Despite their paltry resources, these men did more to hamper the hellish machine of Nazi genocide than did Great Britain and the United States, who were asked to bomb the railways leading to the gas chambers and found excellent reasons to decline.

Passover was coming to an end, an extraordinary week when the party never stops, so to speak: days of rejoicing which the prescriptions of ritual make distinctive in countless ways. And the food, plentiful for once, managed to remind us of pre-war days. It was as if the Passover meal, which is solemnly significant within Jewish liturgy and custom, buoyed up our high hopes. British and US joint forces were completing their conquest of Tunisia. The obstacles they had encountered in North Africa and the extreme slowness of their progress seemed to us less important than the whittling away of the German empire. We were waiting for an Allied landing on the continent, sure that this and the collapse of Hitler's troops were both imminent.

I can hardly remember any point in the war, however dark, when we did not possess the naive certainty that we were only months away, at most, from the Nazis' defeat. These illusions were shored up by the calculations and prognostications of the would-be strategists, combined with the ravings of the would-be oracles. By applying the method used by one of these seers during the First World War, one eventually reached the conclusion that the war would end at Christmas 1942, Easter 1943 or in November of the same year. Nobody was really convinced, but nobody was 100 per cent sceptical either and our crazy expectations held up against the constant disappointments. These puerile hopes took root in a refusal to admit that the war could be prolonged, and the fact that in our situation it was impossible even to contemplate the idea that it could go on. It was possible – only just – to cope with the everyday hardships and the heavy toll of repeated ordeals. But the notion that this hell would be prolonged for long months or years, thereby diminishing our chances of coming out of it alive, was unbearable.

So Passover was ending, the last one that would see us all together, united and alive. Having begun in hope, it finished, one Saturday lunchtime, in disaster. We were about to sit down and eat when the door-bell rang. No one moved. My youngest brother, Jean-Claude, who at that moment happened to be in the corridor, forgot the usual cautionary instructions and opened the door. We heard him exchange a few words with a stranger, then moments later he joined us.

"Papa, there's a gentleman who wants to speak to you," he said.

There was no way my father could hide. He went to speak to the man, was away for a few minutes, and returned in a visible state of anxiety.

"I can't make any sense of it," he told us. "It's someone who works for one of my old clients. He said his boss wants to see me, but when I asked him why, his explanations got very muddled."

Someone had therefore managed to find out where we were hidden, either this former client whom my father had never trusted, or his pre-sumed employee. We made short work of our meal and immediately had a "family council", which consisted of a long monologue from my father, thinking aloud. Only months ago he would still have assessed the situa-tion with his arrogance of old. Seeing his helplessness, it became clear to us that he was a different man entirely. In his view, we were in great dan-ger and could no longer stay in our illicit apartment which had now been exposed. We had to leave without delay. However, there was no way we could find new lodgings immediately. We had no other recourse but to ask friends to take us in. For the first time, the family would be split up. This was an extreme measure which we had never opted for, and now, all of a sudden, we saw it as inevitable. Crushed, we resigned yourselves.

Within twenty-four hours, we were fixed up. Two of my brothers, Henri and Léon, found refuge with the Monheits, a German Jewish couple who had the means to continue living in an opulent apartment which made us envious. Jean-Claude and I were taken in by some old friends who, being elderly and kind, to us were like grandparents. But my father and mother had more difficulty in finding a refuge. Finally a neighbour, a very low-paid worker on the Brussels trams, agreed to give them lodging; his daughter had recently died, so he had a spare room. But there was a very definite proviso: their presence had to be kept secret from the other tenants. The landlord particularly distrusted one of these: a niece who was suspected of sleeping with a German officer and who occupied a room directly above the one where my parents slept. Yet again, there was the nagging fear of being reported.

It so happened that my father fell ill on the very day they moved in. How were they to find a doctor who would treat his inconvenient bronchitis? The Germans had long since prohibited Aryan doctors from the care of Jewish patients, who were only allowed to go to Jewish practitioners, and the majority of these had chosen clandestinity. My father's situation soon got out of hand; his coughing fits could not stay unnoticed and were likely to give him away, particularly at night. He tried to stifle them by burying his head in a pillow, but he urgently needed treatment. The tramway man decently agreed to act as intermediary between my parents and our old family doctor. He went to see him and explained the situation.

"There's nothing I can do. I can't treat Jewish patients." said the doctor.

The tramway man pleaded with him, but to no avail. He came back empty-handed and my father went on stifling his coughs in his pillow. After a few days, seeing the landlord's growing anxiety, he gave up and decided to go. Fortunately, another refuge was found for him and for my mother too.

For my part, I adapted to the situation more easily than I had imagined. Admittedly, the friends who had taken me in now showered me

with affection and I found a way of spending my time by giving lessons
to my younger brother, who was seven. It was pitiful to see him; he cried
a lot, asking for his mother. I was hoping he would get used to the separation and I tried to reason with him and take his mind off it, but I
couldn't manage to cheer him up.

"I'm not staying here," he kept on saying. "I'm going off to look for
Maman. It's not very far and I'll find the way …"

I made an effort to dissuade him, while our hosts gave him sundry
warnings. "You can't go. It's very dangerous! The Germans will catch
you if you go out!"

But he did go out. One afternoon when I had been given permission
to go to a local cinema, and while the "landlords" were having their
afternoon nap, Jean-Claude took his chance. He tiptoed to the front
door, cautiously drew it open, then hurried down the stairs. As soon as
he was out in the street he ran for all he was worth.

He ran for as long as he could, then walked on quickly, driven by
his wish to find his mother. But as he was approaching his destination,
he abruptly encountered an obstacle: the road was cut off by wooden
barriers. Surprised, he hesitated for a moment, but overcame his fear
and started to mount the barrier. Out of breath, sweating and increasingly fraught, he needed several tries at it, but by dint of perseverance
he finally got to the other side. He was hurrying on his way again
when he suddenly became aware of someone at his back, just as a
uniformed man grabbed hold of him. Instantly realising what was happening, he collapsed. They told me so. It's the Germans. It's all my
own fault!

He was wrong. The man was a Belgian police officer who only
wanted to stop him from turning into a road that was closed off. But
when he saw that the child was so distraught, trembling and unable to
speak except for "*Maman, maman …*", he let him go on his way. Jean-
Claude walked on and found himself in the midst of a large crowd

gathered around the Duden Park to watch a cycle race. The spectators were leaning on the barriers or sitting on the ground, talking, laughing, unwrapping their sandwiches and draining their bottles of beer, with all the blithe insouciance of country fairgoers.

Thirty years later, he returned to what he felt that day: "It was as if the war didn't exist there, nor had ever existed. Whereas I, a child, had been experiencing a world of dread and despair. And when I saw those people laughing and enjoying themselves in total ignorance of the anguish I had just been through, it only reinforced that despair. The gaiety of those adults was hateful to me; I had an obscure feeling that they represented the other side of the life from which we were excluded. That was when my tears finally began to flow and I wept as I ran to the house to which my parents had moved. When I got there I threw myself into my mother's arms and she tried to console me. I wanted to shout out: '*Maman*, here's what happened ...'. But I was crying, I was crying and my mother had no idea what was upsetting me. She was saying: 'Don't cry, you're not going back, you'll stay with us.' But my terrible weeping wasn't because of wanting to stay with my parents. I could neither understand nor avow the moral aggression of which I felt myself to be a victim and which was beyond my powers of explanation."

Around 15 May, my father decided that the alarm was over and we could go back home in relative safety. The family was reunited and for a few days we tasted the delights of being together again. Yet from that moment on we were never free of anxiety and we had a growing sense of our precariousness. With the return of the fine weather and the gradual build-up of summer heat we had an overpowering impression that the noose was tightening around our necks. This feeling of disquiet insinuated itself into each one of us. My father lost his self-confidence. Until the day he died, thirty years later, he would never really recover it.

As soon as he was restored to his duties as head of the family – to which
he attached such extraordinary importance – he thought for the first
time about putting his children out of the Nazis' reach. Through the
connections he had maintained with war veterans' networks, he made
inquiries about the possibility of placing us in children's summer camps
or similar institutions. He received an encouraging reply. Forms arrived
with the announcement of imminent departure. To our dread, they were
duly filled in. The success of my father's initiative brought us no joy. We
were caught between the prospect of being split up and an insecurity of
which we were ever more sharply aware.

There were still more formalities to be completed. There were more
and more medical checks, our school outfits were being assembled and,
finally, false identity papers were delivered for my three brothers and
me, which seemed to seal our fates. We were preparing to leave, with
heavy hearts.

And then, abruptly, the whole project collapsed. When we inspected
our false papers we saw that they all contained the same error: systematically, a mistake had been made about our respective ages that made us all
two years older. Today I cannot see why my father had considered this to
be such a serious error, why he had so insistently demanded that it be rec-
tified, and why he finally decided that we were not to go. He explained
that we would run too great a risk with defective identity papers and that
we would compromise the institutions that would be housing us. Without
managing to convince us, he brought us relief. I now wonder whether by
acting like this my father wasn't taking advantage of a fortuitous circumstance to avoid a deadline or to retreat from a separation which, even as he
prepared for it, he dreaded as much as we did.

By way of justification, he had, however, come up with an additional
argument. We had just learned that the Gestapo had raided a Catholic

"Jacques". (Photograph courtesy of the Breendonk national memorial.)

boarding school in Brussels where Jewish children were hidden and had narrowly escaped arrest. One of the principal witnesses to this episode recently told me what happened.

Sister Marie-Aurélie was a member of a congregation in a Brussels suburb where there had been a very substantial Jewish population until the roundups of September 1942. A number of little Jewish girls who had escaped the catastrophe were taken in by the nuns at their boarding school on Avenue Clemenceau. Around the end of May 1943, some Germans turned up, accompanied by an informer whom Sister Marie-Aurélie thought she recognised as "big Jacques". She told me what followed.

"Seeing that nothing could soften the hearts of these tigers, I asked if I could dress the children and give them something to eat before their journey. At this, Liliane, a little girl of four, said to me: 'Sister-*Maman*, are we going so that I can see my *Maman*?' And she clapped her hands, exclaiming 'I'm so glad!'

"The German I'd spoken to told me: 'The children mustn't be frightened; not at all, it's important to cheer them up. We're not taking them to kill them, it's so that we can bring their families together again.'

"There were wails of despair from the bigger ones; they were hanging on to me and asking me not to let them go. At that point big Jacques joined his hands as if in prayer and said: 'Do your utmost to save these children.'

'By what means, Monsieur?' I asked him.

'Prayers, the Cardinal, the King, the Queen … But don't say I told you, otherwise they'd take me; I'm working with them but I'm not for them. They took three of my family.'

"Then, this same man inspected each child thoroughly and pronounced: 'Yes, they're Jews all right.'

"Fortunately, there were three children missing; they'd been baptised at the request of their parents and were in school for the religious education class. And the Germans decided to come back the next day to take away all our Jewish boarders. I made the most of this reprieve to talk to the parish priest, and he advised me to go and see Cardinal Van Roey in Malines. When I explained the situation, the Cardinal said: 'It's best if I don't intervene; it wouldn't solve anything. But do everything in your power to save the children.'"

Armed with these crystal-clear instructions, Sister Marie-Aurélie returned to Brussels. A parish priest who was giving refuge to Jewish boys suggested that she contact Queen Elisabeth, the Queen Mother. The nun didn't succeed in meeting her, but when she heard about the drama being enacted the Queen Mother nonetheless intervened with the German authorities. The Gestapo gave her an assurance that after their arrest the children would not leave the city.

Realising that such a promise was worth very little, the nuns resigned themselves to waiting for a miracle. They were not disappointed. Around ten that night there was a ring at the door. A young man and a young woman belonging to the Front de l'Indépendance announced to Sister Marie-Aurélie that they were taking the matter in hand. They were going to come back with other members of the Resistance to fake an abduction and take the children away during the night. This plan was carried out exactly and the partisans took care to tie up the nuns and lock them in before they left. It was only the next morning that the Brussels police were notified and when the Gestapo arrived on the scene in turn, all they could do was see for themselves that their prey had escaped.

This episode, about which we heard rumours at the time, proved the efficacy of improvised collaboration between Christian charity and Resistance militancy. It also demonstrated that in the institutions where Jewish children found refuge, there was still no shortage of risks and dangers in their situation.

My father therefore decided that we would face these dangers together as a family until the very end.

VIII

It was 8 July 1943. It looked like being a fine day and we were struggling against our desire to go out. My mother was intransigent. For some
time now her growing disquiet had become the source of an authority
she had always lacked before. She still left the house herself now and
then, when she believed it was absolutely necessary. Thus, a few days
earlier, all atremble, she had gone out to shop for food. Within two hours
she was back in a state of distress. It had taken only one trivial incident
to upset her. While she was waiting for the tram, working out the time
she would need to make her purchases and get home, a hand touched her
shoulder. She nearly fainted – "It's my turn, they've come to arrest me!"

It was only a policeman wanting to point out that the tram stop had
been moved. Two hours had passed and my mother still had not got over
her fright. Was the endless anxiety beginning to get the better of her
ability to cope?

We didn't go out on that morning of 8 July; we had resolved to try
our luck once again in the afternoon. We went back to our idiotic games:
an imaginary football tournament and a symbolic Tour de France. But
our hearts weren't in it; the desire to step outside our refuge did not
undo the feelings of apprehension that were always with us.

And then, shortly after the midday meal, the news burst upon us,
brought by a neighbour. Those old friends who had given me lodging in

May, and who for years before that had showered us with affection, had just been arrested by the Germans. The Gestapo had turned up in the middle of the night and taken them away. Added to the deep sense of sadness provoked by their arrest was a suffocating sense of fear and powerlessness. It was not just the extinction of our closest and most devoted friends that appalled us, but the anticipation of our own inevitable misfortunes. The noose was tightening even more.

In 1945, my father had a visit from one of the sons of these ill-fated friends who had been deported. He had spent the war in the Belgian Navy and learned of his parents' death when he came back to Brussels. He asked about how the Jewish community and its leaders had reacted to the persecutions. It was the period of the big religious holidays which packed the synagogues with crowds at the start of autumn. This naval officer went to the one where Chief Rabbi Ulmann was officiating and slapped the former AJB president on the face in front of an astonished audience. His action conveyed the indignation of numerous survivors who, after the Liberation, had expected to see those in charge at the *Judenrat* prosecuted for their connivance or collaboration with the enemy. No legal proceedings were instituted against them. Any initiative of the kind was discouraged by leaders of the Jewish community. One of them justified himself by saying that old wounds should not be reopened and that the Jews had suffered enough. Doubtless, but which Jews? Had the rich suffered as much as the poor, and, most of all, had the accomplices suffered as much as the victims? This was a strange kind of philosophy.

On 9 July 1943, my brother Henri woke up early. That morning he had to go to the town hall of the Schaerbeek district to collect ration cards for some Jewish friends who no longer took the risk of going out. My father stood in front of him sounding off: these formalities were best dealt with really early in the day, before the Gestapo agents said to be keeping watch on the distribution offices got down to work. When he ejected Henri, so to speak, around half past eight, my father was in an extremely nervous state. "Get a move on, hurry up, and be back here as fast as you can!"

Two hours went by and Henri still hadn't come home. My brothers and I were busy in the "playroom"; my father interrupted us: "Did Henri tell you he was thinking of going somewhere else after the rationing office?"

We had hardly seen him before he went out and he had said nothing. My father's anxiety soon got to us. From that moment on the tension kept mounting. By midday, with no news of Henri, it had reached its height. My mother made us take our places at table. She had cooked a vegetable *jardinière* and for once I had difficulty swallowing my food. Even the baby peas wouldn't go down. Halfway through our meal my father got up, unable to contain himself any longer. "I'm off. I'm going to telephone the town hall offices," he said.

The waiting became worse and worse. We couldn't go on eating and we walked up and down the cramped room. My father didn't come back right away. At ten past one the door opened and my father appeared; there were tears on his face. "Our poor Henri, our poor Henri …"

He said nothing else. We all burst out sobbing, and we wept for a very long time. When my father was able to speak, and we to listen, he told us about his telephone conversation with one of the council workers, a former primary school teacher with whom we had maintained cordial relations.

"I saw your son arrive shortly before midday. At the time there were two Gestapo men in the office, sitting in a corner a few feet away from me. Henri didn't notice them and I answered him very roughly, rudely even, to make him go away. But he didn't understand my attitude. Taken aback, he persisted. At that point the Germans got up. They came over and asked him for his identity card. They took him away there and then."

When he heard this news, my father lost consciousness.

Henri, in June 1942.

We didn't immediately think about what time it was when my brother had gone to the rationing office. It was a bit of a mystery. How did he come to arrive there so late when he had left so early? We were soon put in the picture about the reasons for this delay. Rather than going straight away to the rationing office, Henri had first gone to see a young woman whom I knew vaguely. She was the niece of one of my father's friends, a woman of around twenty-five, and as far as I can remember she struck me as an old maid. So we discovered that, without ever telling us, Henri was seeing her regularly. Over the last few weeks his visits had become less frequent. That morning they were together for a long time and when Henri left her he said: "I'm going to catch it from Dad when I get home. He was very nervous this morning already."

Every time I have happened to be in the building where my brother was arrested, to go down the staircase he went down that day with the two Gestapo men either side of him, I have trembled with pity and horror, imagining how he must *certainly* have felt on that 9 July 1943 as midday struck. I have imagined and felt and somehow shared his impressions in the Gestapo car as he saw passers-by making their way home: husbands going back to their wives, pupils coming out of school to be met by their parents and, beyond these banal, everyday encounters, the spectacle of a city whose life goes on, a life continuing while his own has just stopped, dragged into the void and – did he feel it that day? – already seized by death. For years I prayed to God that he would have let Henri go to sleep that night in *his* Dossin barracks, knocked out, stunned by exhaustion, and not seeing us as phantoms the way we saw him.

That same afternoon, my father decided that his son's arrest had to entail ours and that we all had to go and join him at once. I can see myself in the cellar where we were packing. Our father's decision did not disturb us; it seemed natural. Our place was *obviously* beside Henri. Moreover, there was some consolation in thinking that we were going to see him again that very evening, either at the Gestapo headquarters or at the Dossin barracks in Malines. Despair had already given way to a cold determination involving something more than resignation: a sense that the inevitable was finally happening and putting an end to the slow erosion of our courage and the torments of uncertainty. While we got on with our preparations, my father went out. I don't know who he went to, or what they told him, but when he got back he announced that he had changed his mind. I have forgotten how he justified his change of attitude. We submitted without demur. Nor do I know any longer how the day ended. It was a Friday and preparations had been made for the Sabbath. But that day, for the first time, we did not celebrate it. And that night before I fell asleep I heard my father, in the next bed, trying in vain to stifle his sobs.

What became of my brother can be summed up in a few dates. He arrived in Malines on 9 July, as borne out by a record card found after the war. On 31 July, he left Malines on a transport of 1,556 deportees. Only forty of this pitiful cohort returned after the camps were liberated. Henri was not among them. He must have reached Auschwitz early in August and, since he hadn't yet turned sixteen, he was probably sent to the gas chambers straight away.

In this book, I have not asked any questions about myself. That was not my aim. But perhaps I should wonder now why the image of my brother has never left me, and why it becomes increasingly compelling with the passing of time. And what is represented by this child of whom no trace remains? Do his features – engraved for ever in my memory – give body to the countless children who like him have never become men, and men who have never lived out their lives? Is it because he represents a collective tragedy that he has acquired this stature which seems disproportionate to his short existence? For me Henri is not a metaphysical inquiry into the fate of man. My questions about his brief death

Henri's arrest. The Gestapo arrest sheet (left); the record of internment at the Dossin Barracks (right) – the left-hand column shows the dates for parcels received by Henri while at Malines.

throes (whether or not they were really brief: three weeks spent in the Malines antechamber to death, then, with his companions in misfortune, that interminable journey in his coffin on rails, all of them suffocated and crushed for days on end) are put in political and sociological terms. It is in this context that I place his fate and in accordance with these references that I consider his death to be scandalous and intolerable.

He died as a Jew and I have never accepted that anyone should present this death as a willing sacrifice in the service of a cause. He died as a Jew because there were murderers in whose view this condition merited death. He died a victim of anti-Semitism exalted by Nazism and driven to its insane logic. And of capitalism too, which upheld Nazism and whose supreme rampart it was against the "red peril". He died, the victim of murderers and their innumerable accomplices in that European bourgeoisie which armed fascism and gazed without turning a hair upon the tortures inflicted on the members of the Spartakus League, on the miners of Asturias, on Guernica and on the German proletariat. He died because to its monstrous outrages and selfishness was added the weakness of others. He was also a victim of those who did not know how to resist the rise of fascism, who were divided when their unity was needed, who disarmed when fighting was called for. A victim, and so many others with him and like him, of the social and ideological conditioning which delivered them all as lethargic prey into the hands of the executioners. For my brother died without resisting, even though he did not lack for courage; it was just that he didn't know how to fight.

He had the courage that he used up in symbolic gestures like the Remembrance Day demonstrations he organised in the classroom. I know hardly anything else about him in terms of those great confrontations that propelled him towards death. Was he on the left or on the right, insofar as one can be at the age of fifteen? Preserved from any social consciousness, taught fervour but not lucidity, for him these realities did not exist. I have often tried to get to know this boy alongside whom I experienced my childhood, by rallying my scant memories, by questioning the few survivors. But whenever I touch upon this knowledge it all disintegrates, becomes elusive and ungraspable. A few yellowing photographs and my own recollection tell me that he was good-looking and he knew it. His best friend recently talked to me about the teenage love affairs that we only had an inkling of, and I learned from this that life had not denied him everything. He hid his love life from us and this secrecy, of the kind to which people can be driven and closed off from others, was perhaps bound up with his death.

These scraps, not enough to add up to a person, leave me with the mystery of a human being whose presence lives in me for ever and to which, against all reason, I strive to give solidity. When I wrote my first book, I dedicated it to him. This was not out of duty, even though my father asked me to do it. Nor out of some worship of the dead which I have long since given up. I just wanted to take the combination of letters

which make up his name, composed on a page by typography, and give
to my annihilated brother a semblance of existence in some concrete way.
When I had a son I gave him Henri's name. It was not an impulse of my
own and only pressure from my father compelled me to do so. Thank
God, this child has always refused to be called Henri, and for reasons
which are happily not to do with death. Such an impossible identification
would seem sacrilege to me. Henri Liebman has only ever been and only
ever will be that boy of fifteen who was born in Brussels on 15 October
1927 and died in Auschwitz in the early August of 1943.

The next day brought us a consolation which we magnified beyond pro-
portion. Allied troops had managed to land in Sicily. This event
inevitably heralded an imminent liberation. We linked it to the catastrophe of the previous day. It seemed to us that a race had begun between
the forces of good and evil, that the former had just reached a decisive
point and that, with faster and faster progress, they would snatch from
the claws of the Germans the mass of their prisoners in general, and one
in particular. When this offensive got bogged down it quickly brought
us back to a more gloomy state of mind.

As for everything else, we hardly had a chance to organise life anew.
The family had been amputated and we had to adapt to clothes that had
become too big for us. Henri's presence was everywhere and still kept us
busy. We made up parcels for him and every day we took them to the
offices of the AJB, which saw to it that they would reach Malines. We
were living in a provisional state, without any conviction that it would
be possible for us to overcome the shock we had just suffered and turn
ourselves into new people, recreating a collective entity for that family
to which we clung. Was it still a family? In its mutilated form, did it
retain the force of attraction and the power to soothe that had bonded us
together? In the new shocks and upheavals that awaited us, these questions would soon find an unequivocal answer.

On the evening of 21 July, the parcel being made up for Henri was conspicuous on the table. Conspicuous too were the clandestine newspapers that an anonymous partisan had just slipped into our letterbox. I was eagerly starting on one of these when there was an abrupt knock at the door. Immediately, a voice screamed those words which were now almost familiar to us: "Deutsche Polizei!"

Within seconds, two Gestapo men were right in front of us and my mother and I were subjected to interrogation. My father was out and my two brothers were already in bed. My own situation was a delicate one: how could I respond to questions from a Nazi policeman when a clandestine newspaper had just found its way into my hands and was indiscreetly spread across the table? The answer was simple: replies would be given in a somewhat irregular position. Leaning across the table, with my head raised towards the questioner, and my arms strategically positioned to conceal the compromising pages, I prepared myself to speak.

"You get up when you talk to a German!" barked the policeman.

I pretended not to understand and maintained my discourteous but necessary pose. The German was about to pounce on me when my mother came between us and gave me a piece of her mind for my impoliteness. Her intervention fortunately had the effect of a diversion, for her shouting distracted the attention of the two men and I made the most of this to hide my newspapers under a rug.

"Where is your husband?" one of the Germans asked my mother.

"He's gone out."

"You know very well that he has no right. Jews cannot go out after eight o'clock."

"That's true, but he has a special authorisation."

"How come?"

"He is a member of the AJB."

"But in that case, you're protected? …"

"Obviously. Your colleagues have already been to see us and they left us alone."

"Where is your husband's exemption card?"

"He carries it around with him, of course."

"We'll wait for him."

And they made themselves at home.

If my father had come back right then, or if the Germans had not been impatient, we would have been taken away to Malines. But neither of these things was the case. After waiting a few minutes, the two men got up.

"We haven't got time to wait. But tell your husband that tomorrow morning he has to come to the Gestapo offices with his official card. Otherwise, we'll be the ones paying you a visit and you'll be sorry."

Don't let papa come back yet! I kept saying this to myself.

When he did come back, the Germans had left the building. We were saved. But saved only for the time being. We absolutely had to disappear the next day. But where were we to go? We hadn't the faintest idea. It may have been better to sleep on it, but this made no difference to our list of possible refuges. The next morning we were up very early. We wasted hardly any time in getting our suitcases ready. They had been packed ever since 9 July.

We were off! My father had just selected the apartment of his friends the Monheits as the first stop on our wanderings. It was made clear to us as soon as we got there that this had to be a short stopover.

"You can't stay here. Having five more people in the house would attract attention. If you like, you can spend the day with us, but you'll have to leave this evening."

My father disappeared and returned around midday. He had found nothing and left again almost at once. All I can remember of that harrowing afternoon was the discomfort of our hosts. Their bewailings and self-justifications were endless and they kept on saying we would have to leave by curfew. It was a while before my father returned. The atmosphere became more and more oppressive. Every time I went to a window to look out and see if my father was coming back, Monheit would pull me back roughly, shouting at me. "You're mad; people could see you!"

His wife's mother lived with the couple. She was a whingeing old woman who, for all her son-in-law's observations, continually reminded us that we were in the way, that our presence was compromising and not at all welcome. I could scarcely contain myself. Weren't these the people Henri had gone to the town hall to get ration cards for on the day of his arrest?

Around six, my father finally came back. "That's it, we're safe. I saw no end of people and I finally came across Jean Lenaerts. He's going to sort everything out!"

Jean Lenaerts was a wealthy industrialist whom my father had got to know not long before. Before approaching him, he had seen a number of his old friends, none of whom had been either willing or able to help.

My father was bombarded with questions. He couldn't really answer them. He knew only that we had to be out in the street at eleven at night and that we were to go along Avenue Paul Deschanel, where the Monheits' house was. Before we reached the little park at the end of it, "something would happen".

And what if nothing happened?

At eleven o'clock we shook hands with our friends, who were visibly relieved to see us go. We would come back the next day to collect our luggage. There then began a walk of 400 yards, the longest walk in my life. We didn't have very far to go to reach the end of the avenue and we knew that "something would happen" before we got there. A brief and interminable march through the night, and I have never forgotten the mounting dread of it. We were 100 yards, then 50 yards away from the Place Armand Steurs and its gardens and we kept on going, getting more and more worried. We were 40 yards away from the little park. Should be go back to the Monheits? ... They would probably close the door on us.

I was the first to go forward again and the others were following a few yards behind me. I was now level with one of the last houses on the avenue. Beyond it there remained just a few feet of roadway, then the park, in other words emptiness. Then, just as I was going past a big *porte cochère*, I had the impression that it was being opened a little. I slowed down and heard some whispering. A second later, my mother, behind me, was pulled inside by unknown hands. We had arrived at a safe haven.

A stranger asked us to take off our shoes and follow him. He preceded us up the stairs and took us to the first floor, into an apartment plunged in darkness. There were strict instructions not to say a single word and therefore not to ask any questions. We resigned ourselves to being the mere objects of this rescue operation and held our peace until the end, when we found ourselves in beds made up for us. The miracle had happened!

It was confirmed the next morning when we awoke. As soon as we were up, we made the acquaintance of our good-natured and hospitable host, Monsieur Adrien, a printer. Thanks to his hospitality, we suddenly rediscovered pleasures whose existence we had long since forgotten. Even before being put in the picture about our new situation, we were ushered into a dining-room which was the stuff of dreams: it was furnished in a discreetly bourgeois manner, but the breakfast that awaited us was princely. Wide-eyed, we found a table laid with elegance and spread with wonders. There were *white* rolls, butter, eggs, ham, cheese, preserves and *real* coffee served to us by Monsieur Adrien, upon which my mother nearly fainted with happiness. And so one summer morning, the generosity of a leading industrialist lit up fountains of light and life for a few poor, mournful Jews who were one step away from death. And music too, for there was a radio, and the melodious sounds that issued from it bowled us over and melted our hearts, so long had we being deprived of these delights. The songs of Charles Trenet and snatches of *La Traviata* are mingled in my memory of this. It was a dream and we revelled in it.

Monsieur Adrien told us that we would stay with him for some time, though another refuge would be found for us where we would be less exposed to indiscreet eyes and ears. Meanwhile, we were to rest and keep a low profile. This injunction was imperative: we were not to go out at all. Won over as we were by the charms of our new life, this seemed to us a small sacrifice. Our host would take care of reclaiming the luggage we had left behind. As we were discovering the bounty of his apartment – what a lot of books! A new source of joy and delight – he went off to the Monheits to get our suitcases. Half an hour later he was back without the luggage and with some terrible news which revivified our sense of tragedy: the night before, scarcely fifteen minutes after our departure, the Germans had turned up at our friends' door. They had tried to make their escape across the roofs, but had been captured and taken away by the Gestapo.

We had five days of unbelievable peace. Five days of plenty, of music and reading in a house whose light still dazzles me today. But we knew that these days were numbered. It was made clear to us that this oasis had only limited resources and that our flock would have to be dispersed when we left it. So it was like a final holiday and, without ever ceasing to think about Henri, we warmed ourselves in the last rays of our shared sunshine.

It is the third of those five days that strikes me as the most memorable, through its contrast between a late afternoon full of happy excitement and a painful evening. We were overjoyed at rediscovering the delights of the radio and even the German news bulletins held unseemly charms for us. It was during one of these broadcasts, on

25 July 1943, that we learned of Mussolini's downfall. Of course, the *Duce* was neither a German nor a true anti-Semite, so he had never aroused feelings comparable to those we reserved for Hitler; but his complicity with Nazi Germany earned him hatred by proxy. And, above all, didn't his fall from power herald more decisive collapses? It did not take us long to opine that he would soon be dragging Hitler with him into the abyss.

While we were commenting on this wonderful news, Monsieur Adrien told us that Jean Lenaerts had come to see us. But though our benefactor was welcomed with gratitude, he gave us cause for much sadness. That day he had got wind of the news that a transport of deportees was soon to leave Malines. Without explaining precisely how, he told us there was a way he could get letters through to Henri. So we said our epistolary goodbyes. I had hundreds of things to say to him, except for the one that embarrassment prevented me from acknowledging: that he had become dearer to me than ever, that a new kind of attachment had already come into being which would make my departed brother one of the most enduringly-present human beings in my life. In my letter I talked in particular about Mussolini's downfall strengthening his hopes on the eve of his "great journey". Did he receive these letters? Did he find some comfort in them? Whatever the case, he went off six days later. He was fifteen years and nine months old.

And, six days later, the family was broken up too.

On Tuesday 27 July, we had been told that the separation would take place the following day, that my brothers and I were expected around two in the afternoon by new hosts whose identity we were not to know until the moment we met them. My parents, however, would stay on for some time longer at Monsieur Adrien's.

The Wednesday morning was very hard. No longer caring about the books we had rediscovered with such devouring hunger, or the music and the news on the radio, we watched the clock hands advance with knotted stomachs. Our distress was twofold: stirred up and prolonged by the imminent separation, it was made all the keener by uncertainty of what awaited us. Where would we be in three hours' time? In two hours? In just one hour?

For now we were sitting round the table, united for one last time. And together, despite the void of *one* absence that was always experienced physically. There were still five of us, with my mother who nourished us – now as ever – self-effacing to the last in her essential and servile role. Five, counting my father, who was now losing his role. He had ceased to be our protector. He was putting us in other hands. He dared not even look at us. I was fourteen years old, and I had never in my life been parted from my parents. Not for a single day had I escaped from their stifling protection. And my brothers were like me. Except for one small detail, which in their minds was assuming importance and making them different from me. I was the eldest and they trusted me; in the brisk, exuberant and secretive boy that I was they looked for their lost security, the authority of the family and the strength that they themselves lacked.

"Come on, finish your dessert," said my mother, as Jean Lenaerts waited for us to leave the table.

And there we were, standing now. We hugged them. They vanished behind their tears and their inability to speak. We walked out into the street, like robots, but with bad stomach pains. We went inside the austere building that housed a religious congregation. Our first sinister impression was of old women, nothing but old women. We took refuge in the room that was to be ours. There were three of us, just three. Slumped onto our beds, we burst out sobbing and for minutes without end we wept those tears that had been held back for hours and for days.

IX

THEOLOGY HAD NOTHING to do with it, no more than did history: the Catholic religion had always completely terrified me. Among the gloomy figures that had haunted a childhood not lacking in fears, priests loomed large. At the age of three or four I had gone with my father to some patriotic ceremony where there was a religious service. The vast, shadowy church chilled me with terror. Abruptly, a priest came among us, holding a water sprinkler with which he spattered the crowd. I flung myself under the pew and didn't leave this shelter until the mass was over. Ever since then I had avoided processions, which at the time were numerous, even in the city, and I would tremble at the sight of a crucifix. If I turned a corner only to see a *curé* and his acolytes ceremoniously on their way to the bedside of a dying man, I would panic. When I was ten and had to have an operation in a Catholic clinic, and a priest suddenly walked in bringing Sunday communion to the patients in my ward, I very nearly fainted. When I went into the house on the Rue Potagère that was occupied by the Oblate Sisters of Saint Francis of Sales, this time I was entering the Catholic world in my own right.

I had to put on a brave face. Like the nuns around us, I too had souls in my care. My brothers – Léon, aged twelve, and Jean-Claude, seven – clung to me, a fourteen-year-old. There was no question of disappointing or failing them. By chance I came across a series of letters dating from this period and bearing out this determined resolve. Separated for the first time from our parents, we wrote frequently and at length, sending them interminable missives detailing our daily lives, commenting on what was happening in the world, describing our feelings and talking about our problems. I don't think a single day went by without the nourishment of this heartfelt correspondence. For the first two weeks of September 1943, I found no less than fourteen letters written by myself and my brother Léon.

They are a mine of information on every last detail of our lonely and forlorn existence.

We three shared our solitude. We never went out. We saw hardly anyone, except for the nun who prepared our meals and the one who was our teacher, a woman of such a venerable age that it accounted for her faltering lessons. And in the room across from ours, on the third floor of this large building, there was a hard-working woman who came back there in the evening after cleaning all day. She showered us with a kind of baleful affection. She had long been a widow and had lost her only child, a young woman of twenty who had been carried off by tuberculosis. Not content with frequently telling us about it, she showed us photographs of the girl on her deathbed, which took away our appetite for the little treats she gave us at the same time. Such morbid kindness did nothing to brighten up the gloomy weeks of summer 1943.

We knew that our parents were close by. They were living a few hundred yards away, though they did not know our address. We could see the Avenue Paul Deschanel, where they were still being given refuge. "When I lean out of the attic skylight", wrote Léon on 13 September, "and I see Place Armand Steurs and Monsieur's house, I can't help seeing the joke. Your house really seems so close to me it's peculiar to think that we haven't seen you for more than six weeks."

Besides a copious correspondence, our link to them and to the outside world was Jean Lenaerts, who visited us, bringing newspapers and news directly from our parents. We waited impatiently for his visits. Whenever we were left without seeing him for a few days, sometimes a week or more, our anxiety became mingled with an anger which we were very careful not to express. Some visits, however, were disappointing. In his letter of 17 September 1943, Léon noted:

> We were rightly disappointed by the visit on Monday. Monsieur rang at the big street door of the house ... at 20.29. The utter despair reigning over our little clan gave way to an indescribable exuberance; what we were all thinking was: "Monsieur is here, he's come to our rescue". At 8.40 no one had rung for us yet (they ring whenever we are to go down to the ground floor or the kitchen). Still nothing at 8.50, then finally at 8.58, the bell rang on the third floor and, whoosh, we headed down the stairs like the clappers.

But that day, Monsieur had brought no letters, just photos taken in the Brussels districts that were devastated by the bombings. We went back up to our rooms, reassured about our parents but still furious. Another time, Madame Lenaerts came to see us and brought us a big "cramique", a specialty of Belgian pâtisserie that harked back to the wonders of pre-war, and which we hadn't seen for years. We had "cramique" but no letters or newspapers! And Léon's comment: "I can tell you that our disappointment was great and with good cause."

It had the same effect on my parents whenever communications were interrupted. With no news from us for several days, my mother wrote to us on 14 September: "I am so worried today and I am missing you so much, wanting so much to see you that I have a terrible migraine." This was my reply:

> I am speaking to you in particular, dear *Maman*, so that in future we won't have to fret about you. When we're with you again we want our

Chers Parents,

J'étais très content de la lettre de. Papa je vous écris bien, car papa m'a dit que si j'écris bien je reçois une surprise et puisqvous aime beaucoup, papa m'a demandé si je connais déjà l̶ hébreu je connais la cheneneve. J'écoute les conseils de Marcel. Pour demain, j'ai composition de français je dois encore étudier du cc̶c̶ l.. La demoiselle me donne des leçons de 2 m̶e̶ et parfois de 3 e année. Vous savez que notre Léon et toujours le même parresseux il m'̶ ennuie comme avant, Marcel est toujours le même batailleur pour des petites choses. Moi je suis resté un mangeur de soupe, et de légumes il paraît que

la guerre va bien les anglais vont la gagner vite les russes sont aussi très fort
Je vous aime beaucoup
Je vous embrasse très fort

Votre petit
Jean

A letter written by Jean-Claude, aged seven, in 1943.

happiness to be complete; we would be so miserable if we found our dear *Maman* was sick. I understand very well how you must feel, I know it's very hard for you to go for almost a week without any letters at all. But on the other hand you know very well, dear *Maman*, that nothing can happen to us without you being told about it.

In addition to waiting feverishly for letters we also had an extraordinary hunger for news about the world. Newspapers were not enough for us. We incessantly demanded to be told what was in the British radio broadcasts. My father listened to the BBC and transcribed a summary of these transmissions for us. But this didn't deal with all our problems. Léon to his father on 17 September: "I'm asking *Papa* if he can please make sure to set out his reports in a fairly readable way, for it's really pitiful to see our eyesight struggling with the huge difficulties posed by his unreadable writing and unfortunately these battles end to our advantage only rarely." We had a fairly detailed map of Russia on which we could keep track of military operations, but we had to share it with my father. It shuttled between him and us and it suffered from these frequent journeys. We kept on demanding to have a second map, to the point where we tried the patience of a messenger who better understood our appetite for titbits than our hunger for military news.

It was, however, this news that brought us the only joys of which this correspondence retains any record. This applied, in particular, to the events unfolding on the Italian peninsula in September 1943. Léon:

My mind is clear and I can consider the present situation with happiness and an unconcealed inner joy. First and foremost, I must tell you that I am perfectly calm, unlike Marcel, who still hasn't settled down (in terms of his attitude). I have a more or less clear and well-ordered picture of what is happening. Thus, Father Time has given us a big surprise. Indeed, our patience has been rewarded with the long-awaited landings and with them our wild past hopes have become total realities. In life there are these good moments when even the clarity of the brain is not able to convey exactly the often confused thoughts of the mind.

Nor Léon to explain his ideas of strategy in a style where confusion and clarity were completely at home together.

And myself on the same subject that same day:

If we had enough time and if such a thing were possible for us, we would have danced, we would have laughed, we would have done all kinds of mad things, because this day has truly been marvellous, there's no other word for it. How happy I am tonight! I don't know what is stopping me from shouting out my joy to everything around me. It amazes me that here the ladies receive this news so placidly. I don't understand them. Oh, if only we could have celebrated this event together, we wouldn't have welcomed it with such coldness. Oh how lovely the future seems to me, and we are approaching this future at a great pace. Joy is in the air, happiness is in our hearts, life seems more beautiful to me and the burden we bear less heavy.

And I signed it: "your Marcel, optimistic, enthusiastic, trusting and almost happy".

A few days later, we were jolted by some further news: Italy was capitulating unconditionally. Our parents had the benefit of yet another double dissertation.

Léon wrote to them on 9 September 1943:

19.30 hours; the teacher's voice rang out joyfully up the stairwell: "Come down, some good news, very good news". I hurtled downstairs and was beside the teacher in no time. Anxiously, I asked: "Is it a landing?" Instantly came the reply: "Yes." Just then, Marcel arrived and our teacher told us: "Italy has just made an unconditional surrender." She added: "The British radio announced it this morning. But don't get too carried away; it's not altogether certain" … I didn't see any connection between the landing she had told me about two minutes before and the capitulation. From that moment on we were in an indescribable state, so … I won't describe it to you. I'll just say that we were miraculously back up on our third floor ten or twelve seconds later. I was transformed from a "pure philosopher" into a black dancer, a village idiot, a kettle filled with boiling water, an athlete, a clown and I don't know what else….

And ending the letter in this optimistic mood that we had entered once again: "I leave you with the biggest hug ever and for one of the last times on paper."

My own letter betrayed just as much emotion:

Long live joy! Italy, poor Italy has capitulated. This is the news that made us leap and dance and sing. We got it yesterday at 7.30 and right away we were delirious with happiness. Ironically, we were looking at the map of Italy, wretched Italy. I think this time it will be disgusted by such classic stabbing in the back. Oh, they had a good laugh about the dirty trick they played on France. Wouldn't it have been nice to have had Djibouti, Corsica, Nice and Tunisia for Italy. Mussolini was really a brilliant man. And what a brilliant idea of his to team up with the great German Reich. But now, the laughter is over, he had to accept the inevitable, traitors don't always profit from their filthy deeds.

And I concluded like my brother: "Perhaps we shall celebrate Sukkoth at home. But we shall certainly be together for Hanukkah, with Henri and everyone else."[16]

16 The Jewish Festival of Sukkoth is celebrated around the start of October, and Hanukkah during the month of December.

Even Jean-Claude, all of seven years old, wanted to express an opinion: "Last night, we were told that Italy has capitulated. We were jumping for joy, Marcel, Léon and me, because our friends the English are going to win. I hope we'll soon see our family, for we're already very impatient."

Not long after this, the war got bogged down in the West. At the same time we became deprived of our sources of news and we had to look elsewhere for consolation.

In that first half of September there were therefore some occasions for rejoicing and euphoria. They were rare, however, and circumscribed by events remote from the life we were leading. After two months of being kept indoors we wound up reconciled to a life of lethargy. At first we had missed the outside world – to say nothing of the family circle. Later, by force of habit, we accepted the limits of our tiny domain. We would have liked to defend the right to run it ourselves, to organise our games and our reading, to balance out the time between working and day-dreams as we saw fit. But a strict discipline was imposed on us, for the overriding sake of safety as well as other considerations that were less apparently restrictive.

Reduced to total clandestinity, we submitted to such rules without complaining. We could not venture anywhere but the third floor, where we had our two rooms. We were allowed to leave it only when summoned by an electric bell at mealtimes and if we had visitors. These meals afforded us scant enjoyment and scarcely more substantial rations. The Sisters of Saint Francis of Sales had never been inclined to the pleasures of the table and the privations of the war could not have altered their eating habits. We were subjected to the same diet as them; it was unvarying and joyless, at first a source of frustration and in the end provoking our amused irony at its peculiarities. Now and then we were given treats; these and the parcels made up by my mother brightened the dire monotony of this culinary landscape.

As for the visits, I've talked about the impatience with which we awaited them. They were short and intermittent; the reason they meant so much to us was that our visitors appeared most often as messengers. The joy with which we welcomed the ringing of the bell announcing a visit, usually in the evening, was due to our great hunger for letters and news, for the visit itself took place in a stiff and frosty atmosphere to which we never became accustomed. The Mother Superior opened the door of the parlour to us and ushered us in, having first looked us over with a gaze of excruciating severity.

"Come and say good day to your benefactor," she would then invariably say, her words a formula only ever subject to the one alteration, which was when Madame Lenaerts came to see us. Where her husband was warm, she gave the impression of a charitable lady carrying out a social duty – one in which she would sometimes involve her daughter.

We therefore bade good day to our benefactor or benefactress. This salutation with its overtones of gratitude and humility would be followed by an embarrassed silence. The thing was that we hardly knew this man to whom we owed so much and our upbringing had ill-prepared us for social niceties. Our solitude had made us even more uncouth than ever and we would wait impatiently for the interview to be over. At the first indication that the visit was coming to an end, we would get up and gleefully exit from the gloomy parlour with its austere furniture, sombre draperies and countless plaster saints.

I never ceased to feel a childish aversion towards these statues, which abounded in the corridors of the house. Fortunately, we were not obliged to attend the services in the chapel. We were even spared the sight of them, except in rare circumstances whose repetition I dreaded. In our rooms, the tangible signs of religion were limited to a large crucifix. But whereas we avoided the chapel, the big garden outside attracted us. However, in the view of our hosts, its foliage offered insufficient protection against indiscreet eyes, and it was therefore out of bounds. For the sake of fresh air, we had no other recourse but to make surreptitious visits to a small courtyard which was at cellar level and enclosed by high walls. Even our windows were usually shut. In my memory, the summer of 1943, which had begun dramatically, turned out to be stifling.

Safety rules entailed even worse strictures than confinement. Three times a week, cleaning ladies worked their way through the house and our floor in particular. We were locked into our room then and we more or less had to keep still, without breathing a word. There was to be no sound that might give away our presence. Lying on our beds, and taking care not to let the springs creak, we read for hours on end. As soon as the bell rang to let us know the cleaners had gone, by now stiff and exasperated, we would hurl ourselves onto the floor. Having to go without physical exercise was hard for us too. As a remedy for this we had perfected a sports apparatus which gave us scope for some rudimentary gymnastics. This apparatus confined athletic exercise to a form of high jump. Although this was practised without the momentum of a run-up, it was done with spirit, satisfying our inclination for competition and our avid desire for breaking records. For my part, with training I managed to raise the bar to a height of 3 feet 9 inches, jumping over it and bashing myself against the wall of our room to the applause of my two admirers.

Yet again, our reading was meagrely rationed. Of course, the Sisters of Saint Francis of Sales had a library, but, though impressive in size, it confined itself to devotional literature which did not suit us, nor was it even made available. We were reduced to waiting for books that were more to our taste. We devoured everything that was brought to us. *The Count of Monte Cristo* struck us as a downright masterpiece, its quality enhanced by its bulk, and Ponson du Terrail[17] himself in our eyes acquired a stature rarely accorded him by the critics. Since all this was

---

17 Viscount Pierre Alexis Ponson du Terrail (1829–1871), writer of popular serials for newspapers (Trans.).

still not enough for us, we supplemented our reading with whatever we could get, quite indiscriminately. Our neighbour on the same floor had a subscription to *Bonnes soirées*,[18] and thanks to her we discovered another literary genre which was well enough to our liking.

And then, first and foremost, there were our domestic and intellectual chores – the latter being schoolwork. The former were dealt with in no time. We had shared out the basic jobs between us: making the beds and sweeping our rooms. Jean-Claude did his best and turned out to have some aptitude for menial work. But Léon upset our little attempt at a system. I wrote to my parents:

> he is always the same: bone idle. Dear *Maman*, you should see how he makes his bed; it's hilariously funny. Jean-Claude's been doing it for him for a while now. He's also supposed to clean one of the rooms, but when you go to see what he's up to, what do you find? Léon reading in an armchair and poor Jean-Claude, sweating and out of breath, busy wielding a broom twice his size.

Schoolwork was carried out under strict supervision. Our studies were overseen by one of the nuns whom we called "the governess", for reasons that remain for ever mysterious. Though she had a collection of manuals, a severe demeanour and a pronounced liking for authority, her merits ended there and her experience at the job was totally lacking. She aspired to teach us history and geography as well as arithmetic and grammar. In her young days – of which she maintained a fond and distant memory – she had happened to be closely acquainted with a family from London, and this in her eyes was qualification enough for teaching us English. After a few lessons, we were a lot better at it than she was and we generously strove to give her the benefit of our progress.

---

18   A Catholic women's weekly magazine of the period, containing romantic fiction as well as recipes and knitting patterns (Trans.).

In general, her rudimentary teaching methods had ruinous effects. She had a weakness for geography, but she taught it in a way that made us unlikely to share her inclinations. I recall one lesson that she wanted to set us, which consisted in reciting by heart the list of all the tribes in the Belgian Congo. There were eighty of them. Learning the pronunciation of each of these and memorising them cost us superhuman efforts. After a few attempts, we took it up with her, contending that this task was both an impossible and an uninteresting one. She was outraged by what she saw as a challenge to authority, a protest action before its time. As pioneers of a movement that was yet to come into being, we held firm to the end, going on strike and ultimately winning.

Our governess was no less shocked by some homework my brother Léon turned in. For French composition she had set us the somewhat hackneyed topic of the popular saw "the more haste the less speed". Léon decided to treat this major theme in a minor mode. Whereas our teacher was expecting an edifying essay, the composition she received placed the action in a velodrome where a champion cyclist who had taken his prowess for granted was beaten by a humble beginner. With its battery of technical details on the length of gear ratios and bicycle weights, this tale of muscled calves was too much like a piece of titillation for our scandalised governess. She decided to write to my father, but by good luck her letter disappeared amid the unstoppable flood of correspondence.

But the big scandal that rocked our sojourn with the Sisters of Saint Francis of Sales was all because of me. And it came close to ending very badly, when at one point it was deemed that we should be thrown out as fitting punishment for my bad conduct. And it really was bad. In search of new distractions and increasingly reduced to making do with very little, we soon lapsed into fairly vulgar pursuits. A large crucifix was hung high on the wall of our room, its arms held out in an attitude of succour to which we were quite indifferent. It did, however, strike me that here was a target for a competition whose coarseness in no way put us off. The point was to spit to a great height and hit the crucifix, with no ill will intended. This was a difficult task and both Léon and I had to build up to it. By dint of patience (and boredom), our performances nonetheless improved day by day until the time came when I managed to shower the feet of Christ, to the applause of my brothers. Unfortunately, my feat had had not two, but three spectators, for just as I succeeded in my goal, the door to our room opened, making way for our governess. Her indignation was justified and her fury was indescribable.

Half an hour later, I was summoned to the office of the Mother Superior. Her usually austere face had turned icy. I did not even bother to deny what had happened.

"What you did was abominable," said the nun.

I acknowledged this.

"You are going to beg our pardon, on your knees. Otherwise, we shall adopt the most severe measures towards you."

"I won't do as you ask. I admit I was wrong, very wrong. But I won't beg your pardon on my knees," I replied.

The Mother Superior insisted. "You don't realise the gravity of your actions. After what you have done, we can no longer tolerate your presence in this house. You must beg our pardon on your knees."

I repeated that what I had done was shameful, but I persisted in my refusal. I would not kneel down to implore her pardon.

"All right," said the nun. "Go back upstairs to your room. You will soon be informed of my decision."

My brothers were waiting for me in a state of great anxiety. They were fearful of severe sanctions. The idea that we might be thrown out really frightened them. Personally, I did not believe that the Sisters of Saint Francis of Sales would go so far as to eject us. My forecast turned out to be correct and the business ended there. Our hosts' pity had disarmed their devotion.

— —

The cocoon had been re-formed and inside it the roles had been redistributed. Quite naturally, I had assumed the attitude of a father in relation to my two brothers, in other words a vigilant and protective authority. Without actually realising it, I was aping a form of behaviour which perhaps came naturally to me and this model still enjoyed full legitimacy and appeal. Moreover, although my father was absent, he had not given up his prerogatives. I regularly reported to him on the way in which I fulfilled the mandate he had bestowed on me; he replied by giving me advice and what is more by reprimanding my brothers, whom he blamed for lack of discipline.

His severity often took the youngest of us as its object, and in particular the inadequacy of his performance in schoolwork. The letters Jean-Claude wrote to his parents nonetheless demonstrated his perfectly good spelling and painstaking application. But his handwriting did not find favour with either his teacher or his father. He had no trouble taking in grammatical nuances which were usually the preserve of older children, and in conscientiously learning his arithmetical calculations, but he wrote badly and was even worse at putting up with the confinement imposed on him by circumstances.

A letter from me to my father on 6 September 1943:

as for Jean-Claude, he is being set subjects inappropriate for his age: the past anterior, the pluperfect, the future perfect, etc. He copes well, but doesn't have enough supervision. I think I should be firmer with him because he understands that he can take advantage of the situation to get up to mischief. I don't mean that you should think he's naughty; he isn't at all, but like all children of his age he has to be kept an eye on.

I did not do my brother justice, for afterwards my father berated him again, harshly this time. Léon read these rebukes and described in a letter the effects they produced:

> Beside us we saw a flood of tears, looking very sad, oh sad indeed! It was Jean-Claude, mischievous just two minutes ago, and now turning into a public fountain. And to think that for two hours on that same day he had been struggling to come up with a presentable letter and now he was berated for the letter before that and told that he would not be allowed to write any more if he kept up the bad work.

In bed that night, the little boy started crying again.

For all that, the three of us got on very well: by recreating something resembling a family, by cheering one another up, by huddling together and dreaming of the future, we rebuilt the shared life of old; we rediscovered that semblance of warmth that had always made our lives worth while.

And then, all of a sudden, this fragile construct fell apart. Within a few hours, the laboriously built shelter collapsed like the house of cards it had been.

Late in the afternoon of 17 September, Léon was finishing a letter to our parents:

> I have to stop now because something unexpected has happened. We have just been called to be told that we are leaving the house. We know nothing more except that we have to be placed elsewhere by tomorrow. Ideas are going through my head, every single one of them crazy. On the one hand I am happy to be leaving (I haven't seen the street for about seven weeks); yet I'm afraid of our lives being upset, and a new separation.

And he signed: "Worriedly, I send you a hug".

"Worriedly": that was an understatement. We had immediately to be examined by a doctor, we were leaving the Sisters of Saint Francis of Sales for a boarding school and we would be separated, since Jean-Claude couldn't go there because he was too young.

The medical examination took place right away in a building belonging to the *Jeunesse Ouvrière Chrétienne* (JOC), with which we would become so familiar. We were judged to be in perfect health and fit for a stay at one of the "rest homes for frail adolescents" which were run by the organisation.

"What's your name?" I was asked by one of the JOC organisers.

"Marcel Liebman," I replied.

"Very good. From today, your name is Marcel Camara. You are Spanish and you became a refugee in Belgium during the civil war."

We were taken back to our "sisters".

"You'll leave tomorrow," they told us; "tonight you will pack your belongings."

This was purely a manner of speaking. We owned practically nothing. One small suitcase sufficed to hold my clothes, Léon's, a few books and some exercise books. There began an endless evening which left us speechless with dread and sadness. In particular, the thought of leaving Jean-Claude filled me with despair. I had always felt almost maternal towards him, even though his mother's affection had never been anything but unstinting. Within the group made up of myself and my brothers, he and I formed an even more bonded subgroup. The pitched battles in which we good-naturedly engaged had always placed us on the same side, as allies against Henri and Léon. And the last few months spent away from home had forged new bonds between us where my ill-founded severity went hand in hand with an unbounded affection. When he left us the next day, carrying a little bag and with tears in his eyes, I was left sobbing for a long time, as if a piece of myself had been torn off, completing a gradual process of mutilation.

On the same day, despite the dictates of safety, we were given leave to see our parents for a few minutes. It was too brief a meeting to allow any show of feelings. No sooner had we seen them than they were gone. And we were put on a train where, still reeling from our surprises and upheavals, we could ponder at our leisure on what was in store for us.

X

FOR A LONG time I knew nothing about the network that deposited us in the village of Schaltin in the Condroz region one September day in 1943. Here the *Jeunesse Ouvrière Chrétienne* had established one of its "rest homes for frail adolescents". I only came to know the whole story long after the war, when I found out about this organisation that had set itself the goal of saving Jews from deportation and death during the German Occupation.

The *Comité de Défense des Juifs* came into being shortly after the AJB, to which it saw itself as the antidote. It was primarily the initiative of two men: Émile Hambresin, a left-wing Catholic journalist, and Gert Jospa, the communist militant who was later behind the attack on transport number 20 from Malines to Auschwitz in April 1943. He was a member of the *Front de l'Indépendance*, which was probably the biggest resistance network in Belgium, and he took the view that the situation of the Jews required specific action. To set things in motion, he got in touch with his Jewish comrades, with far-left Zionists, and with a number of independent Jewish notables who were within the orbit of the AJB and increasingly at odds with its policy of submission to the Germans. He encountered strong reservations, and sometimes succeeded in overcoming them, as was the case when a university teacher had wanted initial assurances that the *Front de l'Indépendance*, of which the *Comité de*

Défense des Juifs was a branch, was not answerable to the Communists. If this had been so, he would have refused to co-operate with its rescue operation. Thus, in the eye of the storm, pre-war oppositions and resentments remained anachronistically intense. There was even one political grouping, the Bund, a focus for Social Democrat Jews, which refused to join the *Comité de Défense des Juifs* because of the Communist presence in it.

Such sectarianism did not prevent the CDJ from carrying out an operation whose dedication, daring and resourcefulness were of a piece right through the war. Its overall achievements are remarkable: it is reckoned to have saved some 2,500 Jewish children. Acting within the context of the Belgian Resistance, its militants likewise contributed to assisting numerous partisans as well as individuals avoiding forced labour, thanks primarily to the skill they had acquired in counterfeiting identity cards and ration books. In addition to placing children, they also helped Jewish families who had been reduced to destitution. Their money came from different sources: voluntary contributions from patriots and charitable individuals, the "taxation" of certain wealthy people, and the sale of false identity documents. In the spring of 1944, the CDJ managed to involve the big Belgian banks, which paid over the sum of 15 million francs. Admittedly the Liberation was approaching and the bankers had made sure to guarantee that this loan would be reimbursed by international Jewish organisations. The debt was indeed paid off after the war was over. Lastly, the CDJ was a thoroughly underground organisation, taking care of a population of some 10,000 people, adults and children combined.

To save these thousands of children, the *Comité de Défense des Juifs* could rely on the collaboration of numerous Belgian institutions. Resistance workers who had prominent posts in these linked them up with the CDJ's operations. This was the case of the *Oeuvre Nationale de l'Enfance* and a series of Catholic institutions of considerable importance in the life of the country. There were numerous priests and nuns, often acting from personal initiative, who opened up their boarding schools, day schools or convents to a large contingent of little Jews; one of these alone, Father Bruno Reynders, saved some 300 children.

The JOC was one of these Catholic organisations that was active in snatching some of the Nazis' victims away from them. And it was thanks to its discreet collaboration with the CDJ that Léon and I had our first surprise, on the very day of our arrival in Schaltin.

We were leaving the church after Sunday mass, led by our teacher, who had taken us. We were leaving the village when Léon and I saw a group of young people and stopped, dumbfounded. Didn't we know that boy who was walking ahead? Where we had we seen him before? As we got closer, my recollection became more definite and my certainty increased: it was that friend of Arthur's who had gone with him to Switzerland and returned to occupied Belgian after being thrown out by the gendarmes. Just moments before, in church, I had been dwelling on our new isolation.

We are going to find ourselves among dozens of young people, I reflected mournfully, and there will be nothing but unfamiliar faces. We shall have no closeness with them; we shall always be on the alert, having to hide everything from them: our past, our religion, our difficulties and even our name. If at least there were a few Jewish boys in whom we might confide and whose friends and companions in adversity we would become …

And now the first of the boarders we meet at the "rest home for frail adolescents" was a Jew! The delight I felt at this was short-lived. Our young co-religionist was very distant and gave me to understand that he wished to avoid any friendly relationship with us. We found ourselves completely alone.

Alone and lost in a world that was unknown and seemingly hostile. Certainly, this hostility was not openly expressed, but we found its imprint in the total incomprehension surrounding us. The "rest home" was established in a château which looked lovely on the outside. As we arrived, dozens of young people were waiting on the porch for the lunch bell to be rung. Everything about the reception we were given disconcerted us: these new faces, the Walloon accent of these working-class boys, their plebeian looks and the fresh air, the bright light to which we were no longer accustomed.

The first person we spoke to was a blunt-mannered young priest.

"Will it be possible for us to have newspapers here?" I asked him.

He looked at us in surprise. "We never get newspapers here. Anyway, you'll soon make do without them, don't worry."

The good fellow was wrong. This privation was a hard one and the hunger for news gnawed at us unceasingly.

Knowing that we would thus be cut off from the world was the last straw. The substantial meal we were served was not enough to console us.

That first day seemed endless and it was tough. Once lunch was out of the way, a long cross-country walk was announced. We hadn't walked at all for months and that afternoon we covered countless miles. Hand in hand, Léon and I dragged our feet pitifully and were soon left behind by the pack. As the laughter and the martial strains of the Scout songs got further away, we stopped beside the road, our throats dry, our feet bruised and our hearts heavy. For the first time in our lives we had the feeling of being utterly and irremediably abandoned. The room we had occupied at the Sisters of Saint Francis of Sales now appeared like a lost paradise. Would we ever again find the immense tranquillity of there being two or three of us on our own?

In the evening, we went back to the château, on our knees. We went and knocked at the door of the man in charge.

"What do you want?" he asked.

It was very embarrassing for me to put my request into words. I knew it was unusual and I risked not just refusal but ridicule. We had thought about it all afternoon and calculated the chances of success – which struck us as slim – but we judged that we had to take the plunge and save whatever we could of our old closeness.

"We'd like to ask you," I stammered, "if it is possible, or allowed, that my brother and I could sleep in the same bed."

The head man looked at us in bewilderment. To this very day I'm grateful to him for not having made fun of us. "No," he said plainly. "Here, everyone sleeps in their own bed."

Thirty years after we arrived on his patch, he still remembers those two children with the look of beaten dogs. He had seen a succession of Jewish children, many, but none of them had seemed to him so unhappy as those Camara kids who seemed to hold all the world's woes in their eyes.

In the days that followed, we continued to be weighed down by our helplessness. Each day dragged painfully and our sadness only left us in those rare moments when we could get away from the others and forget the community and those in it. After the daily regulation nap, the programme made provision for a half-hour's "free time". It was only then that we could escape the presence of the others. A few hundred yards away from the château, we had found a blessed spot from which it was out of sight. We would sit down on the grass there and unwrap our provisions, or rather our treasure. This was a bag of biscuits my mother had baked herself and given to us just before our departure. Huddled close together, pitiful and ridiculous, we would break this sweet and almost sacred family food into small pieces, treating every crumb with exaggerated respect. The bag of biscuits lasted for a fortnight and every day the same ceremony was repeated until our stock, if not our sorrow, was exhausted. After which, still contemplating the last crumbs of our past, we had to resign ourselves to tackling our new life and looking our companions in the face.

Schaltin in the summer of 1944.

— —

The vast majority of these companions were from working-class families. It was their social condition, aggravated by the privations of the
war, that saw the need for them to spend some time in establishments
where plentiful food, country air and rest would improve their health
and build up their strength. Since there were a great many applications
for a place at the "rest homes for frail adolescents", those selected usually only stayed for a few months, then left to make way for new arrivals.
However, there were a number of boarders who made up a permanent
contingent. Among them were young men old enough to be drafted for
forced labour in Germany and they were mainly to be found in the role
of leaders. And then there were the Jews. There were actually a lot of
them at Schaltin, too many, between twenty and thirty out of a total of
some sixty "residents". In the week after our arrival, they were dispersed across a number of establishments which also belonged to the
JOC. Around a dozen were left, plus the kitchen staff: four Jewish
women whose strong foreign accents risked giving them away, they
were firmly instructed to answer only in monosyllables whenever anyone spoke to them. The most ill at ease was an old lady who didn't know
a single word of French; every time she was asked for something, she
would turn to one of her companions:

"Maggy, salt!" she would invariably shout, whatever the object
requested of her.

Maggy would then come running and, linguistically better equipped,
would make efforts to pin down the overhastily interpreted request.

It was clear that the cooks did not seek to increase their contacts with
the château's youthful inhabitants. They formed a world apart, one
completely foreign to the one in which we moved. In the midst of this,
Léon and I had wasted no time in spotting the other Jews and identify-
ing ourselves to them. These introductions were conducted informally

and were full of precautions consisting as much of irony as of prudence.

A few days after we arrived, one of the boarders came up to us. "Are you two Spanish?" he inquired.

"Yes."

"Do you speak Spanish well?"

"No, we came to Belgium a long time ago, in 1936, and we've forgotten it all."

"Completely?"

"Yes, absolutely everything."

"That's strange. All the same, you've stayed in touch with other refugees or relatives in Spain?"

"No, we've adapted to our new environment and the family was wiped out during the civil war."

"Peculiar. And you're Catholics?"

How could we answer this question other than in the negative when all of our behaviour betrayed our ignorance of Christian practices.

"You aren't Catholics and yet you come to the JOC? Stranger and stranger …"

And our implacable interrogator went off, leaving us feeling extremely embarrassed.

His physical appearance probably suggested that his own origins weren't really Catholic either. But broaching the subject entailed risks we didn't want to run. And how could one attribute so much cruelty or sarcasm to a co-religionist who ought to have understood our torments and shared in them? Some months later, by now well settled in, we in turn participated in this initiation rite to which all the new Jewish arrivals were subjected. There were some who persisted in concealing their identity. Sometimes they were subjected to an interrogation so insistent that they were driven to acknowledge the truth. Despite their confession, they were kept on the margins of a community in the process of being formed.

"Saint François! Joyeux!"

This community rapidly took shape and succeeded even in becoming in some sense institutionally sanctioned. The boarders were divided into groups, modelled on scout patrols. Through gradual approaches, a certain shrewdness and perseverance and some discreet manoeuvring, within a few months we managed to establish a uniformly "Jewish squad". To celebrate this event, we decided to come out into the open. Each group had its own call-sign which it had to shout out at the morning assembly. We had inherited one of these and were not supposed to alter it, but that day we aimed to give it a particular inflection. Impeccably lined up – for once – at the roll call, we shouted out a resounding "Saint François! Joyeux!" pronounced in the accents of the ghettos of Brussels, Antwerp or elsewhere.

This herd instinct which drove us together was fuelled by a powerful nostalgia and a degree of complicity. At night in the dormitory or when chance encounters on a walk made it possible, we would refer to our past and our families. We would reveal our real names. We would talk about wartime experiences and pre-war cooking. The drudgery and duties of communal life held little attraction for us and we contrived to get out of them under the cover of honourable excuses. We soon became known by the name of the "student squad". One of us would work on accounts, one on Spanish, another on English, and I took up Latin. Our enthusiasm varied, but not our reward, which took the form of exemption from certain domestic chores for which we felt ourselves unsuited.

Those above us were no fools. Of course, we were sometimes regarded as shirkers, and not without reason. But there was an understanding of our desire for a closeness with one another and nothing was done to hinder those inclinations in which we found some comfort. In late September 1943 we made preparations so that we could respect the fast of Yom Kippur together. The majority of my fellow Jews were quite ignorant of the Jewish liturgy and it meant little to them. But when we were gathered together for a whole day in one of the dormitories, pretending to be ill, we made up for our lack of orthodoxy with an excess of fervour. I shall speak later about what strange undertakings ensued from the encounter between a "Jewish consciousness" exaggerated by circumstances and the allure of Christian spirituality.

Thus at Schaltin there was a group of "genuine Jews" who, without infringing the dictates of safety, strove to preserve their identity and, even more, to break the rigours of their solitude. However, there were others who remained marginal to the group or made strenuous efforts to ignore its existence. We guessed at their origins and our suspicions were matched by our scarcely concealed animosity and deep contempt. Yet there might well have been legitimate reasons for their stubborn self-exclusion. Caution, for example, might have prohibited them from joining us and they would have been quite right to respect its demands. Perhaps a commitment or a promise given to anguished parents? But we made no allowances and judged them to be lacking in dignity and character. Shortly after the Liberation, I met one of those boys who had been the most stubborn in denying they were Jews. He sported a blue and white armband, as a steward at a Zionist meeting.

Though the early weeks of our stay at the château of Schaltin had been very hard, we soon set about adapting to this new life. Admittedly, it was not without its attractions. For the first time since the war we were eating our fill and this satiety was too novel for us not to relish its delights. The community living which had seemed almost hateful to us in the days following our arrival effected a transformation. We had always lived within the family circle. Henri was the only one of us four brothers to have had any real friends. I myself had been quite happy with the fairly lukewarm camaraderie that bound me to a few of my classmates. In the JOC community, I finally discovered the wonders of friendship.

I was just over fourteen. René P. was eighteen and this superiority in age gave him a prestige all the more considerable from his being the only intellectual of the château's population. He had avoided forced labour; nonetheless, he did not form part of the leadership group and lived on the fringes of the community, in a study retreat which was full of charms. He had a large room which smelled pleasantly of pipe tobacco and, most importantly, was supplied with a well-stocked library. This was where René P. received his young friends and talked to them about psychology, philosophy and, even more frequently, about God, the big topic of the day. He had a ruddy-faced, monklike appearance and his malicious joviality was not without a touch of almost ecclesiastical unctuousness. His education, piety and warmth had made him something of a moral guide for some of us and we vied for his generously given favours. Leaving the other boys for an hour to go to his retreat and confide in him was a source of happiness and pride, marking us out in our own eyes as the enviable chosen few. Those in charge, who were believers but down to earth, viewed this strange boarder not without some mistrust, suspecting him of lapsing into an unwholesome mysticism. But

René P. defied this ill will and went on his way with the luminous smile which doubtless had its source in his dialogues with God. As for myself, I picked up the crumbs from them and those occasional evening walks when my guide would take me alone with him into the countryside, where the only light came from the sparkle of our friendship, I reckon to be among the best hours of my life.

All the same, this friendship did create some problems. I invested it with all the fervour an adolescent can possess, but the edifying and sibylline teachings of Christianity made this very fervour suspect to me. One day, a sermon was preached to us denouncing the insidious depravity of special friendships. In vain I pondered on what this might mean. I ventured to ask those around me some questions, but I took care not to pursue these for I could see very well I was treading on dangerous ground. All I could understand was that a friendship became special whenever it involved two boys and became over-intense. I concluded from this that the feelings I had for René P. were connected to this depravity and that they had to be restored to a more moderate level. I did my utmost, but without success.

A second shadow fell over this exalted relationship. My friendship with René P. displeased a Jewish boarder to whom I had become very close. Maurice L. was a very different kind of person and, in his way, no less appealing than René P. René exuded delight in things. Maurice L. conveyed a deep and expressive sense of sadness. Where the former opened up to people, the latter seemed closed and mysterious. This made me all the more proud at having broken down the wall around him and his richly enigmatic silences. Maurice L. thus became my friend and I became his confidant. Though young, he had experienced tragedies which amply justified his moroseness and made him all the more attractive.

He was the only child of a very poor Jewish couple from Brussels. His father lived from hand to mouth, pressing trousers in a big hotel and gambling away his meagre wages. Maurice and his mother had clung to one another with a passionate and exclusive affection. When the war broke out, in May 1940, his father disappeared without any thoughts of his family and Maurice L. followed the exodus from Belgium. This fourteen-year-old child served as a guide for his mother, a woman paralysed by her ignorance of French. The two of them ended up in the camps where the Vichy government deposited foreign immigrants. They mouldered there for a year before heading back home at Maurice's instigation. On their return they found a father who had lost none of his indifference.

In July 1942, like so many other Jews, the L. family received the summons sent out by the AJB telling them to go to Malines. The father welcomed it without misgivings. He got ready to answer it with a kind of relief, even pleasure. He was sick of his life pressing trousers and he saw departure for the barracks at Malines as an opportunity to break with his exhausting, poverty-stricken existence.

"I'll act sick at Malines and I'll finally be able to get some rest," he told friends.

The mother refused to go and resisted pressure from her husband. She went with Maurice to the AJB headquarters to request exemption but met with only hostility and threats.

The poor woman then resigned herself. She would leave with her husband, but first would save her child. She gathered her paltry savings, went to see a Polish dressmaker and asked her to take care of Maurice. In exchange for a payment of 1,000 francs, the dressmaker agreed.

The separation between the mother and the son was dreadful. Maurice accompanied his parents to the station. His grief was redoubled by a feeling of profound guilt. It was he, he told himself, who had brought his mother back to Belgium from France; it was for him that she had sacrificed her financial resources and submitted to deportation. The train moved away from the station platform, leaving behind a ravaged and soul-destroyed young man.

His miseries were only beginning. The Polish dressmaker treated him as an outsider. He lived on the margins of the family. Solitude impelled him to keep a bitter diary in which his landlady did not get off lightly. The diary was discovered and its author thrown out. For months he wandered from refuge to refuge and plied a variety of trades. A grocer who had given him a job wanted to make him look after his horse. Maurice refused and had to clear off. He found work in a bookshop, but when his boss learned he was Jewish he made his apologies for having to dismiss him. He worked in a cardboard factory and was forced to make a run for it when the Gestapo unexpectedly turned up with "big Jacques" leading the way. Finally he ended up with a family at Waterloo where other Jews had been given shelter. It didn't take the Nazis long to come down on them. Maurice managed to hide in an attic, along with a young girl. When he heard the Germans on the stairs, he hid his companion in a big wicker basket and escaped through the skylight. He found himself on the rooftop just as it was being battered by a downpour and to this he owed his safety. He stayed there for an hour or two, numbed by the cold and shaking with fear. That was when he started his first dialogue with God.

"If you save me, I'll believe in you," he swore.

The Gestapo discovered the young girl in her basket, but the deluge put them off venturing out onto the roof. Maurice was saved. He believed in God with a faith that was ferocious and aggressive, absolute and ephemeral. This drew me to him and gave our friendship a religious, missionary aspect which I shall speak about later.

And so there was friendship. There were also classroom alliances and camaraderie, and games and life in the open air which gave us an appetite we were at long last able to satisfy. Moreover, a spirit of brotherhood existed, for in the "rest homes for frail adolescents" the Scout tradition did not stand in the way of an atmosphere which ruled out authoritarianism. We also had the strong impression that we were relatively safe. We felt we were out of reach of the Gestapo and we were protected from the aerial bombing of Belgian towns and cities that had become ever more deadly since the winter of 1943. Of course, the war continued to be an ordeal for us, particularly the uncertainty about what was happening to our parents. We knew they were in the countryside with Jean-Claude. But sometimes months went by without our receiving any sign of life from them.

From Léon to my parents, 25 April 1944:

> We are still waiting for news from you. The last letter was dated 28 February and if maybe you are worried, we are likewise just as much, and wearied and I don't know what else. Every morning, when the letters that have come are handed out, our hopes are renewed, and every time we have a fresh disappointment. I don't understand this stubborn silence.

We were not to say any more than this so as to prevent the likelihood of a censor guessing at the extent and basis of our fears. When a letter did eventually arrive, we melted with happiness, expecting the reappearance of that long impatience and searing anxiety. I can recall an afternoon I spent at Ciney, our closest town. Walking alone through the streets, I glimpsed through the window of a well-off-looking house a family gathered around the table. I was hit by a huge wave of nostalgia. The town had just undergone a violent bombardment whose traces were still apparent.

What do these devastations and dangers matter after all, I thought. Give me back the happiness of being with my family and I would gladly put up with living under the bombs.

So the ordeal continued and anxiety never wholly released us from its grip. To cope with this, we had discovered a resource hitherto unfamiliar to us: it was in Schaltin that we found God! This was the key event of that last year of the war and for a long time it turned our lives upside-down.

Of course, I came from a family where religious ritual had been practised a great deal and where belief in God was a part of everyday experience. From my earliest childhood I had maintained a daily dialogue with him. Prayers took the familiar form of extremely prosaic requests which boiled down to a cursory and more or less routine liturgy:

"Good morning God! Don't let me be asked any questions about grammar and let everything go well in the gym lesson. Goodbye God!"

Otherwise, our religiosity had more to do with family ritual than spiritual experience. Prayer itself was not really something we knew: instead we had the reciting of almost incomprehensible Hebrew formulas.

A few months with the JOC's "frail adolescents" was enough to transform us. Without any induction from the vicars and sub-vicars of the Lord, we surrendered directly and with little resistance to the heavenly archangels themselves. To a greater extent than anyone else, a number of Jewish adolescents, of whom I was one, acknowledged and assumed this metamorphosis. From then on we were possessed by an all-devouring faith. It gripped us and transported us with enthusiasm, intoxicated us, consumed us with a fire which in some cases took long years to be extinguished. Very few Jewish boys escaped this religious fascination. Everything impelled us towards an open susceptibility. The ordeals we had undergone made for an extremely favourable seedbed, and at our age we were ripe for transcendent and uplifting experiences. Bigotry would probably have put us off, but there was no trace of it at Schaltin. There, the practice of Christianity was certainly regular and even lavish, but it didn't descend into any narrow-minded strictures. We had to be present at mass every morning but during it we were allowed to read our own books provided they were relatively edifying. I can remember one of these which was a collection of meditations, and a title in it that struck me. The title was *Lenin*, and the topic of it was dedication and self-sacrifice. It described the Russian revolutionary's modesty, his humility and the austerity to which he remained faithful when he reached the summit of power. The conclusion became clearly lodged in my mind: "Lord, enable me to serve You with as much self-denial as Lenin brought to the service of Satan." This was my first encounter with the founder of Soviet Russia.

Those who ran the "rest home" displayed the utmost liberalism in relation to the Jews. The only person who ever talked to me systematically about God, and without falling into Christian apologetics, was René P. When he spoke, it was only about the great spiritual virtues, which were largely identified with the practice of introspection and with altruism. The name of Jesus was never pronounced, nor that of Mary or any saint, nor were any articles of Catholic dogma. Our meetings were bathed in a Franciscan spirit of beatitude shaded only by a touch of manliness. And while the *"poverello"* was not the beneficiary of a cult, there was instead a contemporary figure who held a major place in our conversations: Father Vincent Lebbe, a Belgian missionary established in China and, in his way, playing a part in the great movement for decolonisation, since he had worked hard all his life to pull the Catholic Church out of its Eurocentrist conditioning. However, what impressed me, more than the fact that he had managed to have a few Chinese bishops consecrated by the Vatican, was his philosophy of life. It could be summed up by three great principles which seemed to me the key to happiness as well as heroism: true charity, total renunciation and unceasing joy. To which was added this dictum which struck me as a fundamental and revolutionary truth: one had to be happy not *in spite of* everything but *because of* everything. I must confess that the most luminous aphorisms of Marx on the class struggle or socialism never made such an impression on me as these Franciscan-inspired maxims did at the time.

Any crude proselytising would certainly have put us off, but there was no sign of this from our hosts. The lay people at the top were not in the least interested, taken up as they were with their organisational and teaching roles. They even saw René P. as abusing his status by talking to us about God and thought he should have avoided this topic completely. As for the large number of priests who passed through the château in succession, they were no less reserved. The chaplain in particular was well liked by everyone because of his smiling, fatherly discretion. The JOC's "rest homes for frail adolescents" had been made the responsibility of a Jesuit and the clerics we met belonged for the most part to the same order. This gave to an establishment initially designed for working-class residents a bourgeois colouring which ruled out any references to social problems or the condition of the proletariat in, for example, sermons, lectures (which were anyway fairly infrequent) or speeches. What was lost on the one hand was, however, gained on the other: the refinement of the Jesuits made for a climate of benevolent and flexible tolerance.

Conversions were extremely rare events. I can recall only two instances: that of a young miner from the Borinage[19] who was solemnly baptised at the age of fifteen, but whose devotion was short-lived, and that of the Jewish teenager whose religious convictions were more lasting. He belonged to the "student squad" and we regarded him as one of us. But he was less inclined to criticism and discussion than we were, and more readily receptive to that Catholic dogma to which we remained impervious – even in our quasi-mystical crises. We were nonetheless very surprised to learn that he had decided to convert. Some of us viewed his decision as a betrayal. I for one defended my companion against the sometimes vehement accusations by insisting on freedom of opinion. The chaplain guessed at our unease and called all the Jewish boarders into his study. This was the only meeting of that kind, and he told us that no pressure had been exerted on our companion, that he understood our feelings and our reservations, that he came close to

---

19 The Borinage is the region southwest of Mons, straddling the French frontier, and once a
    major coalfield. It was the setting for Zola's influential novel *Germinal*. (Trans.)

sharing them, but that the young man had so much insisted on being baptised that he had deemed it his duty to bow to his will.

In this atmosphere of temperate and fervent religiosity, I think there was only one single virtue intentionally preached to us: chastity. Purity was often spoken about to us and it was always identified with abstinence. Since the age of the boarders ranged in general between fifteen and eighteen, some of our moral guides judged it necessary to talk to them about "preparation for marriage". This they did in veiled terms, becoming explicit only in the matter of condemning masturbation. For this there was no indulgence and no forgiveness. Our responses to these expectations and anathemas were not all the same, but we were all equally troubled. One of my Jewish classmates who had left Schaltin to pursue his studies in a private school wrote to one of the priests:

> As for the point on which you have asked me to do better, I have kept the promise I gave you and have in fact achieved a real triumph of will: for two months I have not deliberately erred a single time. It still happened to me recently during the night, but it happened while I was asleep and I am not responsible.

It seems that the merits of chastity were no less vaunted in the school than at Schaltin, and the slightest failings of this kind, or any situation which was likely to give rise to them, were repressed with a virtuous severity. In the same letter, my classmate thought himself compelled to justify the very poor assessment he had achieved under the heading of "conduct": "In the marks for the first week, you will observe a 2, which happens to be the same as X; he had come to my cubicle without permission to ask me for a comb." I don't think it was vanity that these rigorous educators had wished to sanction.

I for one enjoyed more peaceful nights and our dormitories did not possess any troubling cubicles. But there can be no doubt that from the fund of Christianity which I long preserved it was the "hatred of sin" that proved most enduring. The maxims of Father Lebbe had long since been shelved when I was still being haunted by a horror of lust and impurity.

The young Jews of Schaltin were more bewitched by religion than were any other boys. Among them were some who had experienced an atmosphere of traditional observance in their families. There were others who came from a-religious backgrounds, and these were more numerous. All of them followed an identical route whereby they discovered a new sensibility. With rare exceptions, no one formally adopted the Catholic religion, no one even dreamt of taking this step. This rejection contained a twofold feeling in which fidelity had as much and even greater a share than critical thinking. The Catholic religion seemed to us sublime but it remained essentially foreign. As for me and Léon, we quaked at the very idea of having to own up to our parents about a possible conversion. My father was not without anxiety on this point and he conveyed it to me in one of his letters. Tactfully, I strove to reassure him. In December 1943 I wrote to him:

> One more thing … in your letter you remind me of the promise I made on 21 June 1942 (this being the date of my religious confirmation as a Jew). There is nothing to fear, I still adhere to the promise of fidelity. I understand your fears about this: that "what has happened to many others" could happen to me. But I, or rather we, are of a different calibre and "that" will never happen to us.

Aware though we were of the duty of fidelity, we nonetheless felt the need to distance ourselves from a past in which the religious aspect had been more or less absent. How were we to reconcile these contradictory demands? By dint of pious and imaginative reflection we found a solution. This was how the JIN, the *Jeunesse Israélite Nouvelle* (New Israelite Youth) came into being. It is Maurice L. who must take credit as its founder. He spoke to two of his Jewish friends and succeeded in persuading them. He came to me later with the same success. I became number 4 in the "organisation", and there was never a number 5.

The philosophy of our project took shape in the course of our walks and the conversations we kept up even in the latrines. What we were learning daily about the Old Testament had convinced us of its inadequacies. Catholic teaching displayed a traditional contempt for the Jewish religion and used the word "Pharisee" as implicit condemnation of its formalistic dryness. Those of us who were familiar with Jewish religious customs confirmed this harsh judgement. Nothing could be less like a living, vibrant faith than a ritual which left little room for spiritual feeling and mystical fervour. So our duty was clear: to regenerate the beliefs of our ancestors by taking our inspiration from the prestigious Christian model. Writing to a Jesuit priest shortly after the Liberation, Maurice L. eloquently commented on the undertaking he had initiated:

> You gave me a glimpse of something other than the material world and of aiming for a goal much greater than merely getting along in life without doing any harm and without doing any good. Instead of doing as other companions of mine have done in seeing the beauty of the Christian religion and comparing it to the decline of the Jewish people, and opting to change their religion, acting selfishly when all is said and done (since this way they save only their own souls and leave the people in ignorance), I have formed a plan to bring back the chosen people – who have, however, strayed through certain traditions and a way of life unto themselves – to what they were thousands of years ago, which is to say a people loving, praising and glorifying God.

And poor Maurice L. added:

> I know that I have already been called all sorts of names because I had
> this plan: "arrogant", "a madman", "a crank"; but I don't care and I
> continue to believe that this is where we must begin to bring about the
> "regeneration of the Jewish people" and, with God's help, I hope to be
> able to contribute to that regeneration.

At Schaltin, no one had called Maurice L. a crank. Admittedly, there
were only three of us in on his secret. But we had no doubt that it was a
happy combination of idealism and good sense which only had to be
established in terms of practical means of application. Since our group
had been unanimous about the aim of the enterprise, it remained an issue
to be dealt with in some kind of statutory manner. It was the subject of
numerous discussions which never lacked for seriousness or passion.
The first point we had to settle concerned the missionaries of the New
Israelite Youth. One very straightforward question bothered us and in
the end it divided us. Should these men devoted to the service of God
follow the example of Catholic priests and take the vow of celibacy?
The models that we observed daily and the edifying homilies on chastity
with which we were favoured made us come down on the side of
celibacy. Only one of us, Samuel Friedmann, defended the differing
point of view. We had no trouble understanding him: of all the JIN
disciples he was the one most susceptible to the charms of girls, and at
Sunday mass he was the only one of us giving them the eye. Moreover,
he was the same one who gave his spiritual director an account of the
nocturnal battles to which his heroic virtue compelled him. He pleaded
for the right to marriage, but in vain. He made us resort to a vote for the
sake of settling this historic debate; by three against one we decided that
rabbis would henceforth be constrained by celibacy and chastity. Samuel
yielded democratically and went on eyeing up the village girls.

Samuel Friedman, in the minority over celibacy.

We had yet more set-tos. How could this be surprising? We had to resolve numerous crucial issues: would it be appropriate to rebuild the temple at Jerusalem, or not? Should the animal sacrifices which the Hebrews once practised be re-established, or not? Should we focus our project on Palestine? Vigorous debates and heated opinions were the rule in our association, but they did not affect the feelings of brotherhood that the members of the sect swore to one another.

However, like any sect, the JIN had its splits and, like any sect, it experienced a rift from which it never recovered. The cause of this was straightforward and had nothing to do with the mission we aimed to accomplish. The reason for it will be deemed pointless: I myself, playing a decisive role in this sorry business, regarded it instead as being of vital importance. Maurice L., whose moral authority had never been called into question, discredited himself in my eyes because he had expressed some sharp criticisms of René P. At the time when this unforgivable error was perpetrated, he was at a school some way away and discharged his tirade by letter. I replied with a missive from which certain passages remain in my memory. After telling him that our friendship and our collaboration were impossible from now on, I entreated him to give up his participation in the JIN and hand it over to me. I don't know what my claim is based upon and I can only recall the conclusion to my letter, written in capital letters: "Despite everything, I maintain my trust in you. I am sure that you will withdraw and you will realise that the fate of seventeen million Jews lies in your hands".

Thus the JIN ended. The temple at Jerusalem was not rebuilt. Rabbis continued to get married and Maurice L., forsaken by everyone, for some time pondered yet more great thoughts and noble projects without ever regaining the audience he had won.

It was early August 1944 and we were in the middle of the holiday period. The boarders at the château had seen a strong contingent of summer residents arrive and among them was Samuel Friedmann, who had escaped from his school and to whom I was having much difficulty in explaining the reasons for my break with Maurice L. He did not hold it against me, for we now viewed the JIN question as having lost its importance. Our thoughts were elsewhere and our hopes clung to more immediate prospects: the US forces had just broken through the German front at Avranches and had begun a steady progress which intimated that Liberation would soon come. This time our hopes *couldn't* be disappointed. Already, euphoria was taking hold of us, along with the certainty that our ordeal was near its close, that we were witnessing our deliverance, that the dangers had been surmounted and that the ending of the nightmare was now just a matter of days. The dream, the great dream of liberation, the mirage of safety, of homecoming, of happy reunions, was all assuming substance already. We felt the first tremors of the overflowing joy that this miraculous event would bring us. Peace was there, in the air of this marvellous summer, on the horizon, around the bend in the road, within hand's reach, like something grasped already and already fondly touched. We had it in our fingers, palpable and quivering. Peace and freedom.

On 4 August, around nine, when the morning assembly had just finished, I went up to a room which was used as a study, and opened my Latin books and exercise books. I had just written a few lines when I was startled by the sound of cars roaring past. At the time it was unusual for a car to go by and was something of an event. I rushed to the window, glanced outside and stepped back in horror. The Germans were there, shouting incomprehensible commands and bursting into the château. I walked out into the second-floor hallway and ran into a Jewish classmate. We stayed there for a few moments, listening carefully and trying to make sense of what was going on without venturing downstairs.

"We shouldn't go down," I told my companion. "If they come upstairs, we should lock ourselves in the toilets. Or else we can escape over the roofs."

"Do what you like. I'm going down to the ground floor!" he said. He was shaking like a leaf and he looked distraught.

"You're mad! They'll arrest you! What have you got to lose by staying here?"

"There's no point. We've had it. We might as well give ourselves up!"

I begged him to do nothing, not to abandon me. In vain. The poor fellow had lost his head. He left me, went down to the entrance hall and surrendered to the Nazi police. For my part, I lay low in my room. Was it one hour I stayed there, or two, ready to throw myself under one of the beds if I heard the Germans coming? Time seemed endless and the situation desperate. At any moment, I expected to see the Gestapo make their appearance and seize hold of me. But the minutes went by and each quarter of an hour was endless. Only the noises in the house and some shouting confirmed that the Germans were still in the château. When I heard the sound of yet another engine, I didn't dare look out of the window, for fear that this roaring announced not the departure of the Germans, but the arrival of more police. After all this agitation, a great silence pervaded the place. Yet I stayed glued to my bed. This caution saved me, for soon after this a car backfired; it was a second German car arriving with reinforcements.

It was very late when I ventured out of my hiding place. Carefully, I went down to the first floor and soon found my hopes confirmed: the Gestapo had gone. It was only at this moment that I thought about my brother Léon. What had become of him? Had the Germans arrested him? And my other classmate? I rushed down to the ground floor. Léon was there, in the hallway, waving up to me furiously. I hurled myself into his arms, out of breath. And where were the others?

"They arrested seven," Léon told me.

And he described the dramatic events. Hardly had the Germans entered the château and burst into the chaplain's study than everyone was assembled on the front steps by one of the policemen. Some minutes later, one of the Gestapo came and stood in front of the group, scanning the boys' faces inquisitorially. Beside him was the young Jew who had been frightened to death and left me to give himself up to the police. He was of German origin and had gone completely out of his mind; these two reasons sufficed to make him accept the role of interpreter and intermediary.

Addressing his words to his classmates, he pronounced: "That's it, we've been found out. It's futile denying it. They've come to look for seven Jews and I'm the one who must point them out. If I don't, they will take it upon themselves. And now, I'm going to translate everything the officer says."

And he translated: "The young Jews are to step out. It's a matter of honour and loyalty. Why are you hiding here anyway? Because you are cowards, hypocrites, parasites and idlers. Now you are going to leave for

Germany where you will be put to work. It will be a new life for you. I won't deny it will be pretty hard, but we will treat you decently."

After which, the wretched interpreter pointed out seven boys. Among them there were six Jews, including Léon, and a young "Aryan" man who could be recognised as such.

The six boys were separated from the rest and had to present themselves in a drawing-room where other Germans were waiting for them. When Léon went in there he had the presence of mind to pronounce: "I am not Jewish. I am Spanish and you have no right to arrest me."

To his enormous surprise, he heard one of the officers reply: "In that case, excuse us. The Spanish are our allies and we have the greatest respect for General Franco. You may go."

Flabbergasted, Léon complied.

Another of the young Jewish boys managed likewise to dupe the Germans and was immediately released. Four boys were taken away, among them Samuel Friedmann. After which, furious because they had not managed to find the seven Jews they were looking for, the Germans took their revenge by arresting three of the people who ran the rest home. All of them were deported to Germany. One of them died in the camps. Of the four Jews, Samuel Friedmann and the hapless "interpreter" suffered the same fate.

A month after their arrest, Schaltin was liberated by American troops.

XI

EXACTLY A YEAR after we arrived at Schaltin we left the château to go back to Brussels, which had already been liberated two weeks earlier. We got there the next day, too late to take part in the popular jubilation. The flags were still at all the windows, but the fairy lights had gone out.

Those first days and weeks as a family and in freedom were what we had dreamt of for years. Nothing in our imagination could compare with them. The story of the Liberation had to be a return to joy or even just to life; every hour would be savoured for what it was: a profound relief, tasted for what it would be: soothing tranquillity. And happiness would be an everyday thing, with all the added pleasures of life: the cinema again, and the city to be rediscovered, and comfort to be regained, hunger satisfied and, most of all, the bonds of family renewed. My narrative would be incomplete if it did not recall the reality of Liberation: a huge disappointment. Not content with its own abominations, the war corrupted the peace that put an end to it.

The same day that I returned to Brussels I had a presentiment of this unbelievable disappointment. I found myself on a train that was taking us from Charleroi to the capital. As in May 1940, we were travelling in cattle wagons, sitting on the floor with our legs dangling into the void. Around me, the boys were laughing and next to me Léon seemed radiant. I, however, felt a sense of great unease. I was going home, I knew my parents were alive and Jean-Claude would be there too, and yet I was not happy. The moment we came out of the tunnel, I almost missed the darkness that had repelled me; the moment I touched the ground, I felt a kind of nostalgia for the storms that had buffeted us. I was sad and I was ashamed of my sadness.

From the station, we rushed to our house. In a fever, but joylessly, I pushed the doorbell. There were footsteps in the corridor. The door opened and we were greeted by a stranger. He had no idea where my parents were. For nearly a year he had been the occupant of their apartment.

We ran from one neighbour to the other to try and track them down. Finally we discovered that they were staying on the other side of the city, with friends of long standing. Another dash across Brussels and, at the end of our journey, an unfamiliar house out of which my father suddenly appeared at the first ring of the doorbell. Upon the sight of us he let out a loud cry which brought my mother running. When I saw them I was not so much delighted as disturbed. My father had aged and he seemed less happy than he should have been. That very morning he had been hit by some distressing news. The friend who had taken them in was a German Jew who had been married for a very long time to an "Aryan" woman. It was because of this that he had not been bothered by the occupying forces. But after the Liberation he had been arrested by the Belgian police in the wake of a ridiculous denunciation. My father had gone to great lengths to secure his release and had achieved this the night before. The poor man was due to come home on the day of our arrival but had been struck down by a heart attack during the night. We found ourselves in a house of mourning.

We stayed there for a week, enough time, we thought, to recover our apartment. Unfortunately, the occupants refused to leave it. Having settled into a house for which we were paying the rent and with our furniture in it, they were quite happy and intended to prolong their stay. While we waited we moved into a shabby furnished flat where my father fell ill. His illness held up procedures and it took us several weeks before we could get our apartment back.

These were also weeks of idleness. We were in a hurry to get back to school, but didn't dare turn up because we were totally bereft of suitable clothing. It was not until the end of November that we put in an appearance, and we were little noticed. Only one single teacher took the trouble to say hello to us; only one inquired about what had become of Henri. Lessons resumed in a frosty atmosphere: it was as if we were in alien territory. The pupils around me had no time for a boy of such pathetic appearance, two years older than them and clearly out of his element in a role he was no longer familiar with. Things went from bad to worse when I displaced the boy at the top of the class in the first compositions.

Our poverty was overwhelming. It was exacerbated by a sordid legal business. During the final year of the Occupation, my parents had been hidden by some farmers with money troubles. A price had been set for their board at the start of the stay, but soon after this my father was given notice that the charge was being raised. He lacked the means to pay this and refused. With the threat of reporting him to the Gestapo, the farmer compelled him to sign an IOU. As soon as the Germans had gone, he demanded that the debt be settled. My father balked at this until the day when a judge told him he was liable for payment. We narrowly escaped the bailiffs and seizure of our property.

Early in the winter, my father was appointed head of a centre for the location and repatriation of deported Jews. It was an honourable and useful employment, but the salary was derisory, so we suffered from hunger and especially from the cold. Every week I would go to Antwerp where there were cousins – the only relatives left to us – who had a store of coal. To get to their house I would go through the Jewish quarter which I had known when it was full of life; now I had a dismal walk through a desert peopled by ghosts. At the time the city was under perpetual assault from the notorious V1 and V2 bombers and I would spend the night in an atmosphere of terror. The next morning I would leave for Brussels again with a 55-pound sack of coal on my back, travelling with it along the tracks and makeshift bridges of the dilapidated railway as far as the station at Berchem. We would have heating for a few days, then go back to shivering in expectation of the next trip to Antwerp.

We were totally destitute and our moral fibre was no less impoverished. A few days after my return I had a long conversation with my father. I told him that during my year of "rest", I had given a lot of thought to my future and that meditation had helped me to decide on the certainty of my vocation: I wanted to become a rabbi. He gave a start.

"A rabbi! What are you thinking of! It's a profession for good for nothings!"

I tried to tell him that I intended to work flat out to become a rabbi, as I would later in the exercise of my duties. I spoke to him about God and about serving others. He replied that this was all nonsense, that it was foreign to Jewish traditions and that I had to free myself of Catholic influences.

Our first serious discussion got us nowhere. Something snapped between father and son. Had he changed as much as this? Had the war turned him into someone in whom influence had been replaced by authoritarianism? Or was it that I had opened my eyes to hitherto unsuspected failings? Was I not alone in feeling this degradation? The family's isolation increased. Most of our old friends had been deported. No new ones appeared. The family home lost its warmth.

During that autumn of 1944 I felt appallingly alone, as if upon the ruins of a wrecked family and a thwarted vocation, cut off from the youthful community which had transformed my existence for a whole year. On 31 October, I wrote to the chaplain of the JOC "rest homes". It was a dejected and impassioned letter which conveyed a keen religiosity all the more heightened by my new solitude.

The atmosphere of your pastoral care, which was so warm and friendly, most of all so religious, exerts a very salutary influence upon souls that wish to be uplifted. If today I have a better understanding of my duty as a Jew, as a child of God, if today I am firmly decided upon giving myself entirely to the service of God and my people, it is thanks to its influence. And that is something I shall *never* forget. If I manage to fulfil my vocation, to achieve my aim, if at the end of my life I can say that I have done my duty and carried out the Holy Will of God, I shall remember that this was very much thanks to your care. I came into your care weak and I leave it strong; I came into it with no ideals, I leave it with a splendid one; I came into that care without God's Goodness, and I leave it with Him.

At Christmas, when the Germans were launching their final offensive in the Ardennes, I was gripped by an enormous nostalgia: I remembered the feast we had celebrated in December 1943. I went to the church to pray in solitude and for some months I assumed the habit of going there when there were no services on. In it I found a peacefulness that was absent from synagogues and a comfort that no other place could offer me. Soon after this I experienced great happiness when, after having tracked down René P., I went to Leuven where he was studying, found him and fell into his arms.

This was a real post-war reunion. There were no others. From April 1945 onwards, deportees were returning to Belgium. Transports brought back survivors of the camps. None of us ever stood on a platform in the hope of seeing Henri get off the train.

And I do not remember ever having wept for his absence and his death during that year of 1945 which knew no springtime.

XII

THESE THEN ARE the shadows of death; here then are my ghosts risen from a past where I thought I had hidden them away for ever. Time should have wiped away their traces. The opposite has happened: these figures are more present than ever. Is it my age that draws me into this exploration of my childhood? The present has also played a part in this look back at myself, since for a lot of men and women who lived through the war, the fashion for the look of the past, what one might call the "retro style", goes against the grain. Its description of the upheaval offers a seductive lie which makes meretricious the half-tones and pastel colours of a period less banal than the present time. The Belle Époque has, so to speak, extended its empire and annexed the interwar period, and even the Second World War itself. The desire to debunk and demystify has led to new forms of mystification: there were neither victims nor executioners, there was neither resistance nor collaborators, neither cowardice nor heroism – just a display of human mediocrity heightened by a few poetic touches, courtesy of the artist.

In its way, my story is a reaction against this travesty of history with its wish to obliterate the crimes of some and the complicity of others, and also to annul the (often belated) raising of consciousness or spirit of rebellion and resistance that gave a response to those betrayals and abdications. As for "the phenomena of class", people just prefer to see these as a matter of old ideological habits in need of straightening out. But it would take some doing: these distinctions that the war respected and reinforced between the weak and the strong, the rich and the poor, the bourgeoisie and the proletariat are not easily rooted out of reality. The fact that I was a child masked these distinctions from me, but it did not protect me from them.

They made me suffer an injustice which, in the very midst of Jews as a persecuted group, made distinctions between the affluent and the poor (the latter handed over defenceless) and set its notables, for the most part of Belgian nationality, against the immigrants, the undesirable plebs. I was only indirectly aware of the anti-Nazi struggle, yet this struggle was happening around us. Let us simplify its outlines: it was a struggle between left and right. The "retro style", in common with so many other lies, is a pretence that they did not exist. And yet even raking through the history of that petty bourgeois family of mine, so wretched and unaware, I can find echoes of a confrontation that at the time was unapparent but fundamentally important.

There is not just "retro style". There is something else and there is more: my shadows, my ghosts, my dead have all been brought back and have been set against me like so many reproaches and accusations as the conflict in the Middle East has increasingly plunged Europe into passionate divisions. As a Jew – *although* a Jew, as people say all too often – at the time of the Six Day War in 1967, I took a position in favour of the Palestinians. What made it worse was that I took it publicly. This seemed to me to be my right. I was given to understand that it was a betrayal. I don't want to go into the death threats I received, as did my wife and my children. The spectres of the war had nothing to do with it. But there were those who took it upon themselves to revive them.

I was lecturing one day in front of an audience assembled by the RTB, the Belgian broadcasting network. On the agenda was the Israeli–Arab conflict which I and my debating opponent, the future minister Gol, were attempting to elucidate. Our arguments were exchanged with extreme courtesy before an attentive and apparently calm group of listeners. Only apparently. When the debate was over, three ladies came up to me and, without a voice being raised, spoke these very words: "Monsieur, we find it a great pity that you weren't gassed in Auschwitz."

This was the first throwback to the darkness of the past.

Not long after this, I was speaking to an audience of students who were divided for and against the state of Israel. The atmosphere in the room was tense. It soon became disorderly. I went so far as to describe what Palestinian refugees were going through and to present them as what they were: innocent victims. This had the effect of an intolerable provocation. There was a clamour and one of the shouts directed at me was: "Jacques!"

Many of those present that night did not know what this meant. Those who have followed my story know which criminal the comparison was meant to refer to: the monstrous informant who, despite being a Jew himself, had decimated the Jewish community in Brussels during the war.

This was the second throwback to the darkness of the past. A third soon came on its heels.

One of the Jewish newspapers in Antwerp thought it worth entertaining its readers with some Jews who were critical of Zionism and the policies of the Israelis. In my case, the reporter, not having bothered to quote any of my opinions since he deemed that a caricature of these would do just as well, concluded his diatribe in the following terms: if this man had had the opportunity, he "would undoubtedly have been one of the Nazis' most loyal henchmen at Auschwitz".

Auschwitz again. And I won't dwell on what became commonplace abuse: "traitor", "renegade", "anti-Semite". My "betrayal" came down to those few written or oral statements whereby I believed I expressed my political convictions. For example,

An alliance must be brought about between Jews and Arabs to combat all the consequences of chauvinism and to recognise the reality of the Israeli nation.

Or

The phrase "destruction of the state of Israel" (which the Arabs often used before 1967) is dangerously ambiguous. If what it means is the extermination of a population, it is an altogether abominable solution. The Arabs have a duty to make it clear that the project of extermination which is quite casually attributed to them is utterly alien to them, and that Israel as a national entity has the right to exist.

Later:

We must ask ourselves whether Israel's integration into the Middle East, which is indispensable for the establishing of a lasting peace, will ever prove possible so long as the Jewish state refuses the status of full citizenship to some of its nationals, the Israeli Arabs, for the simple reason that they are not Jews. A solution to the situation in the Middle East is only conceivable if Israel chooses the route to peaceful integration into the region where it has settled, by gradually taking the appropriate measures to diminish all the conditions of discrimination between Arabs and Jews which it has set up by virtue of its Zionist nature. Such a perspective would of course entail the abandonment of the fundamental premises of Zionism. But if this were the price to be paid for the survival of millions of Israelis, individually and collectively, who would then take responsibility for rejecting it, and even, as is often the case, refusing to consider it?

These writings are both commonplace and extraordinary. They call Zionism and Israel's policies into question, an unforgivable error at a

time when the pro-Israeli passions of the majority of Jews aim to dis-
courage any criticism of the Jewish state. But their condemnation makes
no difference to me. My socialist convictions dispense me from any
respect for states in general, even the Belgian state, of which I am
nonetheless a national. I am not a citizen of the state of Israel, which is
all the more reason why I have no duty of allegiance to it. My opinions
on the Middle East situation, moreover, express a humanism, an interna-
tionalism and an attachment to peace which make no claims to
originality but bespeak my personal history and the manner of conversion whereby I detached myself from an unduly protracted childhood
and from the Jewish traditionalism in which it had been steeped.

The Liberation had returned me, excited and chilled to the bone, to the
paternal home. Without ever recovering its tepid allure, the family environment regained an anachronistic and austere ascendancy. We had been
radiant children. We became rigid teenagers. The family that had once
been open now turned in upon itself. Added to the severity of traditional
Jewish custom was a puritanism that we owed to the Catholic influences
we had not recovered from. This had as much effect on our opinions as
on our way of living. In the "Royal Question" that divided Belgian not
long after the war, my sympathies went to Leopold III.[20] The day of his
abdication was a day of mourning. I went to meetings of the Social-
Christian Party. This shocked a lot of our Jewish friends, who
mistrusted the Church and who were, at the time, very susceptible to the
charms of the Soviet Union. A double wall protected me from the left.
A fervent religiosity set me against Marxist materialism and my father's

20 As Commander-in-Chief of the Belgian Army, in 1940 Leopold III gave an unconditional
surrender to the invading Nazi forces. This was against the wishes of the government (which
had withdrawn to France). After the war, Leopold's conduct was the subject of controversy
– the "Royal Question" – which led to a referendum on whether he should return to rule the
country. The outcome was only narrowly in his favour and he abdicated, leaving the throne
to his son Baudouin (Trans.).

situation made my anti-communism all the keener. He had resumed his professional activities, but the Czech firm he had represented before the war had now been nationalised. This had not improved its efficiency and my father came up against an inert bureaucracy which in our minds quickly became synonymous with socialism. In 1948, the "Prague coup" upset us as if we personally had been its victims. I saw in the Cold War the bases of a holy war and during the Korean conflict I was very much vexed with myself for not volunteering to defend the Free World.

At Brussels University, I thought I could repay my debt of gratitude to the Catholic world. In this institution dedicated to free inquiry and anti-clericalism, the Royal Question and the first skirmishes in a new phase of the education war were vigorously exercising people's minds. "Churchy" students were tolerated so long as they agreed to shut up about their beliefs. This discrimination towards a minority had the effect of bringing me close to it and – yet again! – made me take refuge behind a rampart of spirituality. All this became reconciled with a form of Jewish practice that was traditional, familial and superficial in its religious implications, while bearing a greater burden of political and psychological meanings. The cocoon had been re-formed.

I was twenty by the time I began to suspect its existence. Then, all too slowly, I became aware of it and set myself to shake it off. I realised that if I were to free myself of it I would have no alternative but to take my distance. When, with my university degree in my pocket, I decided to pursue further studies in England, the intent was less to refine my knowledge than to liberate myself from family constraints. This move away was all it took for me to see the world with different eyes. I also discovered Marxism. I was helped in this by a London academic, Ralph Miliband, whose strength of conviction was devoid of any dogmatism. This was no sudden revelation, but much rather a matter of progressive recognition. It equipped me with a method of analysis, one which was heir to the old rationalist impulse, and political beliefs which I would have wished to be more militant. For me, the shabbiness of the Stalinists' reformism and authoritarianism ruled out joining the socialist and communist organisations. I resigned myself to being merely a left-wing intellectual whose commitment was confined to narrow tracks: historical research and intermittently, whenever the occasion arose, an activism tinged with idealism. Thus, for example, I took part in the movement launched, in Belgium as well as in France, for the cause of Algerian independence, secretly at first, then in a public way after I was "exposed".

I had gradually set myself apart from the Jewish community, doing so without either passion or acrimony: a detachment rather than a rejection. My path took me towards new allegiances which now gave me a closeness to comrades rather than co-religionists. As for my religious faith, it did not shatter; it withered and well and truly died: slow death throes which spared me any suffering. My Jewishness itself was on the way to becoming unspoken, then I was brought back to it through the roundabout route of politics.

During the Algerian war, the FLN was anxious to have the Jewish community stay on, even though they were increasingly tempted to leave, and they asked me to be an activist in this area. It was a matter of mounting an action that would promote coexistence between the Arabs and the Jews in the Maghreb, at the same time as the Zionist movement was urging the latter to migrate to Israel. I was not at all drawn to this activity and agreed to take it on only out of regard for discipline. After trying to persuade progressive Jews in Belgium, I realised that the success of my task was impeded by the limitations of a community with little influence. In London I made contact with Labour MPs. As unofficial plenipotentiary, I embarked on negotiations of a kind with the World Jewish Congress. I wanted to make it share my conviction that a rapprochement between Jews and Arabs in the struggle against French colonialism could contribute to breaking down Israel's united front with

Western imperialism, to improving its relations with its neighbours and to promoting the peaceful establishment of the Jewish state in the Middle East. It did not take much perspicacity to discover how precarious was the alliance between Israel and France, which was waging the most unjust of wars in North Africa. And since the Algerian FLN was canvassing the co-operation of the Jews and was moreover visibly moderate in its views on Israel, there was a historic opportunity to be seized. Nahum Goldmann left me with no illusions. In the Geneva hotel where we met, he told me virtually word for word that what interested him was an agreement with Nasser. "The Algerians are too revolutionary." Nothing came of this discussion.

So the Algerian war was my first encounter with the Arab–Jewish problem. It led me, without my having wished for it, into involvement in political actions as a Jew, even though my deep motivation had nothing to do with this particular consideration and was rooted in my anti-colonialist convictions.

Experience showed me the damage wrought by the anti-Arab racism of some Jews. Appalled, I had also observed the development of an unconditional pro-Israeli stance that paralysed a great many Jews, even the progressives, over the question of distancing themselves from Zionist policies.

The outbreak of the Israeli–Arab war of 1967 prolonged this situation and amplified it beyond anything I could have foreseen. Left-wing groupings were then very much at a loss: they wavered between their sympathy for the Jews who had survived the war (and therefore, by implication, for the state of Israel) and their opposition to the Western imperialism which triumphed with the defeat of Nasser. I was known to be increasingly critical of the politics of the Jewish state. I was questioned about my reactions to events. I was asked to speak to militants, to prepare a manifesto which would go against the grain and modify the wave of pro-Israeli feeling which was visceral for some and sentimental for nearly everyone. My own aim was to keep a cool head, and protect the right to rational political analysis along with the priorities of social-ist commitment. In the Jewish community, I have not been forgiven for this. Nor was my father forgiven for it.

He was, quite naturally, deeply attached to Israel, but out of affection as much as curiosity he agreed to hear me out and even questioned me on my opinions. He was not persuaded but he acknowledged the sincer-ity and coherence of my positions. Perhaps he had been impressed by my initiative on a visit to Cairo in 1969, when I approached Anwar el-Sadat, taking up the cause of hundreds of Egyptian Jews who had been imprisoned during the Six Day War; I succeeded in bringing about their release. Faced with a stream of accusations mounted against his son – "traitor", "bastard", "hireling" (detailing the fabulous sums that I was supposedly receiving from the Arabs because I defended the Palestinians) – he would become indignant and defend me. He was banned from the synagogue he went to. When he died, the Kehilatenou newsletter of the Brussels Jewish community refused to publish the short obituary usually bestowed on its deceased members. One of his best friends, a prominent figure in the community, had agreed to give a brief homily. He spoke in the room where my father had died. The coffin was in it and all around my two brothers and I, various relatives and friends were packed together in a room that was too small. There was the customary recollection of the merits of the deceased. Then, suddenly, this curt pro-nouncement: "it is a great misfortune that Monsieur Liebman's end was precipitated by the enormous grief he felt because of his son's betrayal." This deliberate lie left me flabbergasted. The truth, however, was that my father's end, if not exactly hastened, was certainly shadowed by the bad feeling which pursued him even in the Jewish nursing home where he was cared for in the last months of his life.

Before I was set against my father in an imaginary opposition, I had been set against the memory of the Jewish martyrs of the Nazi persecution and, in particular, that of my brother. I have often been heckled like this: "How can you attack Israel and defend the Palestinians? Don't you think of your dead, your own people, your brother?"

On the contrary, I think of them very much. My reading would remind me, just as would my teaching work, were there any need. And the city where I live, peopled with memories and dear to me most of all because my brother lived in it, along with some others whom I will never forget, other faces I endlessly picture in my mind. I often think of this dead brother of mine and other victims of the same crime. But questioning corpses is an obsession I shall leave to those for whom it is a vocation. I have no faith in the virtue of these false dialogues. The answers attributed to the dead do not issue from them. Finding justifications in these is either a paltry consolation or a massive fraud. I myself will settle for questioning history. It is hard enough already to make it speak, to distinguish it from legend, to disentangle the skein of events and extract some lessons and surmises from it. In a broad and indirect way, this is what my book has had in mind. As I reach its conclusion, I can imagine the reader's surprise: yours was the condition of being a Jew, that "Jewish situation" in which you are still placed today, and in your early life you endured those tragedies which are prolonged even today by this ambiguous status; what does all this mean to you, and is there not some need for you to explain it? What does it mean to you now to be a Jew?

"Seeing oneself as a Jew" is not about affirming an "identity" that goes beyond any other consideration, in some absolute sense. One is not a Jew above every kind of social standing, every kind of philosophical choice, every political opinion. On the contrary one's way of "being a Jew" reflects all of these factors, even when one claims to be ignorant of their existence. My own way is that of an intellectual who has made the choice of becoming a Marxist. It is that of a socialist who has adopted a stance of refusal towards capitalism. Individuals can't be chopped up into multiple characters; an individual is a whole, full of contradictions of course, but a whole.

My "Jewish baggage" is a historical baggage. Although its origins go far beyond myself, it consists first and foremost of my own history, my own story. I've told enough of it for no one to be in any doubt that it has left its mark on me. Is it to be defined by a culture, which in itself is heterogeneous, or a background: that reassuring albeit fragile family in two minds between keeping to itself and being open to the outside world? A culture and a background expressed through countless different realities: folk music and synagogue chants, perennial festivals unfolding with their soothing rituals, traditional cooking (which Jews well know draws its flavour at least as much from an emotional atmosphere as from any inherent qualities), a humour tinged with irony so aptly allied to the warm intonations of the Yiddish tongue; perhaps too a variety of humanism which in its way conveyed and sublimated the weakness of a community that was prey to every kind of danger. And these dangers themselves, which shape the plot of our histories and which permeate the tortured psychology and muddled ideology of so many harrowed, anxious Jews.

To this should be added an additional circumstance. I belong to a pivotal generation and a period of transition. Like many Jews of my age, I experienced the world of persecution and marginality; we were the sons and daughters of refugees and are now integrated into a more open society. The traces of anti-Semitism have not entirely disappeared from it, and they sometimes take the form of varying degrees of prejudice and a mistrust that is to a certain extent not overt. But it is a declining evil; nowadays racism picks out the more defenceless victims that are to be found among immigrant workers.

The old poverty of the deracinated Jews has given way to an undoubted prosperity: the Jews have become bourgeoisified. For a great number of them, this social reality has been accompanied by a political phenomenon. As the sociologist Hapgood puts it: "the intellectuals of the ghetto were to a large extent won over to socialism". The poverty of the Jews, both in the East and West, had the effect of bringing them close to the left. As they have increased their income they have moved away from it. And, moreover, their past sympathy for a progressivism basically identified with the Soviet Union did not hold up against the revelations of Stalin's crimes. Those more to the left, those brought into the fold of "the party" through the anti-fascist struggle and the Resistance, then brought down to earth, bitter and disappointed, have most often been the ones surging back towards the right and finding a source of comfort in their attachment to the state of Israel.

For this generation, the "Jewish experience" – if one means thereby a series of specific behaviours in the way of life, language and environment – is becoming attenuated and increasingly a matter of psychological and ideological data. The Jews are less and less confined to particular occupations, which weakens one of the main sources of their homogeneity. This development gives rise to a number of contradictory promptings: should the memory of the harm endured be cultivated, out of fidelity; or should the work of time be encouraged to heal the traumas and close the wounds? In political terms, this alternative can be expressed more or less like this: should the specific characteristics of the "Jewish community" be reinforced, cementing all its precise features, protecting a heritage handed down from the past and defending it all against the "dangers of assimilation"? Or should there instead be a wish to pursue the progressive work of integration of this community, so that barriers may be eroded and distinctions effaced?

The great majority of Jewish institutions, be they religious, social or political, have a very clear position. Not only have they chosen the path of particularism – not to say nationalism – which is their most basic right, but they also condemn assimilation and denounce it as inherently criminal. For them it is nothing but the culmination of the Nazis' attempted extermination: Jews, the Hitlerites wanted to murder your bodies; the "assimilationists" want to murder your souls! This frequently advanced comparison is a feature of the lowest form of demagoguery, since those who have recourse to it do not even believe in it themselves. If they did believe in it, they would have to propose the same sanctions for "assimilationists" as for war criminals! The debate would acquire greater clarity if it were to be rid of such excesses. Unfortunately, they still have a good deal of currency. Not long ago, I met a Jewish student who was so carried away by his own words (which contained not the slightest trace of cynicism) he professed that if maintaining an "everlasting Jewish identity" had to be at the cost of "a new flare-up of anti-Semitism and a new Auschwitz", then this price would have to be paid. Let the Jews perish for the sake of preserving their "soul"!

This is an extreme expression of the position. It should not be held against the opponents of assimilation. But can't one ask the reasonably minded proponents of "everlasting Jewish identity" – of the "upholding of the Jewish people" – what they understand by it and by what means they intend to achieve their goals? Is it the defence of Jewish culture, which is necessarily different from the national Israeli culture, even though linked to it? What does it mean? Will "Jewish culture" still be spoken of when the Jews who live in Western societies are becoming less and less distinct from the national communities where they are established? They no longer have their own language, or any customs which are specific to them, or – except in some cases – dietary rituals which are strictly theirs, and their religious practice is now adhered to only by a minority. These gaps are meant to be filled by the cult of the past and the exaltation of "Jewish values". But one would be hard put to define these outside the social context that gave rise to them and which has now disappeared.

As long ago as the 1950s Margaret Mead observed that in the United States, the world's greatest Jewish population centre, Jewishness (*Yiddischkeit*) was a culture which no longer existed except in memory. Is there a current wish to recreate it, and by what means? The only possible route would be through segregationist practices of which some examples can still be found today: concentrating Jewish children into private schools, drawing them into youth movements which are exclusively Jewish and, above all, the prevention of "mixed marriages", presented at best as a defection, but all too often as an out-and-out betrayal. In every respect, stressing the differences between Jews and non-Jews, emphasising them, giving them validity, exalting them and reinforcing the divisions whenever there is any tendency to their attenuation, reproducing them when they become diminished.

There are claims that this apology for Jewish particularism can be legitimately defended on the grounds that it is akin to regional cultures. Yet there is one difference between them which I see as fundamental. Protecting these cultures against the centralisation which denies and destroys regional riches is not something which leads to people being isolated from their colleagues and neighbours, and children from their classmates; on the contrary, it reinforces the bonds that unite them and ends the solitude that threatens them. But the language of Jewish particularism – not that of regionalism – comes down to these formulations: defend your cultural heritage by cutting yourself off from your fellow students, your workmates and your neighbours, because you are different from them and you must remain so. And if, in answer to these pleadings, people were to ask what is the nature of this difference, they would hear this answer: it's true that you speak the same language as your non-Jewish neighbours, that you listen to the same music as them, that you face the same problems, that you are subject to the same laws and the same authorities, but your *past* is different; preserve it; that past is sacred. If need be, to find an "identity", go back to it. This endlessly reiterated argument is not without consequences. How many young Jews who have known nothing of the wartime persecutions are thereby led to the painful ambivalence of a marginality which is experienced like a rupture from their environment. One of them recently told me:

"I was born in Belgium and have always lived here, but I cannot flourish here: I have no sense of camaraderie or friendship or love between myself and the Belgians with whom I rub shoulders every day."

This is an extreme example, but it is not exceptional. And this too is part of the "Jewish heritage", along with the humour and the humanism.

One objection frequently raised which can easily distort the argument is this: So you want to ban Jewish particularism?

Not at all; I don't like interdictions. They are usually odious and for the most part not effective. But whenever any reinforcement of particularisms – outside the present context and through an ideological discourse focused on the past – threatens to separate Belgian Jews from Belgians who are not Jews and French Jews from French people who are not Jews ("be different from them, cultivate your differences!"), I have a foreboding of certain danger.

It is not intellectual speculation which reveals the nature of this danger to us, but a reading of history, of my history and that of the Jews in occupied Belgium. Remember the case of Gert Jospa and a number of other militants who were the founders of the Committee for the Defence of the Jews. In their social relationships and political choices, the majority of these men were not particularist Jews cultivating and exalting their differences. They were Jewish immigrants (an objective and not ideological circumstance) connected with Belgian working-class organisations. This fact was not incidental to their initiative, an initiative which resulted in the saving of 2–3,000 Jewish children as well as numerous adults. None of the institutions which were part of the "community", all of them proudly displaying the Jewish label in terms of either nationalism or religion, came close to this achievement. And how many of those in charge of them, speaking in the name of the communities they led, lapsed into an over-dignified impotence or a shameful collaboration, into class selfishness and a xenophobia which took the "Jews from the East" as its victims? In this overview of the majority of the traditional Jewish institutions, whether in the matter of resignation, abdication or complicity, their actions were most often the result of a social isolation which the Nazi occupier criminally aggravated and exploited. The heroism of the Jewish partisans, acting in concert with non-Jewish partisans, is sufficient proof that it is not lack of courage which explains the passivity of the majority, but their marginal situation within Belgian society.

Compared with the traditional Jewish communities, Zionism appears to be situated on more solid ground. It openly advocates that Jews leave for Israel to live in a state that is their own. Thus they would be protected from the double hazard of assimilation and the persecution which the Zionists have often claimed is inevitable. This is a radical point of view which is not without coherence. Zionism has an additional merit: it puts an end to the weakness and the ideology of resignation in which the Jewish communities had enclosed themselves, and from which the only ones to escape were the revolutionary combatants: Eisner, Rosa Luxemburg, Trotsky, Radek, Zinoviev and so many other Jewish militants, socialists and communists.

Unfortunately for it, Zionism nonetheless comes up against a twofold objection which events themselves endlessly lay against it. Setting itself the goal of giving Jews a haven of peace, Zionism has created a state which has never ceased to be fraught with insecurity. The reason for this is simple: situated in a region which powerful interests have always coveted, Israel was also founded on the plundering of the Palestinian populations, who were rapidly reduced to the condition of displaced persons or second-class citizens. Whether or not one regards an injustice of this kind as the price that inevitably had to be paid in reparation for the crimes of anti-Semitism, it is futile to deny that injustice. Its consequences forever hold Israel's survival at stake. That country's own citizens present it as a citadel under siege.

In its attempt to gather the whole of world Jewry into a single state, Zionism has been no more successful. But though it does not manage to attract a great number of immigrants, it is more effective in its aim of persuading the scattered Jewish communities that they must see the state of Israel as a true homeland, one to which they are bound by overriding obligations, from that of unconditional political support to that of financial assistance to the point where it has been qualified as a "tax". As for the Jewish youth, it is invited to reach the old "Promised Land" and told repeatedly that it will never "come about" in either France, the US or Belgium – to say nothing of the USSR. Once again, this can entail and does indeed entail reactions of anxiety, tension and withdrawal ... but not necessarily departure. Thus there is yet another, extremely perilous drawback to the particularist stance: not content with aiming to recreate their cultural differences as much as possible, the Jewish communities may similarly present themselves as centres politically bound to a foreign state. Are not the seeds of a new anti-Semitism to be glimpsed in this? Admittedly the Zionists, who have long deemed it inevitable, would be more easily consoled than others and would find in it confirmation of their gloomy forecasts.

But, I am frequently quizzed, will your children be Jews? I get an urge to answer this with: leave my children – and yours – to follow their own inclinations. We are Jews, and I am one, not as the bearers of some message or some culture, but as the bearers of a past. A Jew is someone who holds within him a Jew's history, a history he has experienced and that should not be one he has learned from books or sermons. Why shouldn't our children's experience, which you want to lock up inside Jewish history, the Jewish past, be that of boys and girls who are freed from the spectres of yesterday and who desire a freedom expressed in the terms of today. "Jewish culture" and the ordeals of their parents are one of their many and varied aspects. Why should the blinding lights of yesterday's conflagrations be beamed straight at them? Yes, yesterday.

Shall I be taxed with dangerous optimism because I do not believe in the inevitability of racism in general and of anti-Jewish hatred in particular? What I do believe is that these scourges will not disappear naturally but need to be fought against actively. The vicissitudes of this struggle may justify exile in certain circumstances. But the systematic exodus that Zionism advocates seems to me to offer no solution: it uproots, it maims, and it leaves the field to the enemy.

Yes, to the enemy. Any obligation I have felt to the dead of the war and, if one wished to personalise this, to one of them in particular, is a duty that comes down to this: holding the racism that murdered them to be a crime in which one never colludes. Racism is insidious and creeps into the most ordinary human relationships; it is sly and besets even the finest minds; it is cunning and decks itself out in good justifications; it has an unusual potency, so that it often contaminates its own victims and pits its chosen targets against one another. This last observation, though widely applicable, has pertained for far too long in the case of the Jews and the Arabs, whose antagonism is in so many respects fratricidal.

In my cruelly imaginary dialogues with my brother Henri – who stands for and embodies millions of murdered Jews and also (why not?) for gypsies and Armenians, blacks and so many others – I will speak in no other terms but these: in murdering you, racism hacked out a void that will never be filled; the survivors themselves have been stricken. I bear this mutilation which is your presence in me. It is a wound that could be bitterness and a shrivelling into hatred and a wish for revenge. These states of mind do not tempt me. If the Nazis had killed you when you were not so young, my memory of you might have been tinged with less harshness. But in depriving you of all the good things life still had to offer, they left me no other recourse but to bring this memory to some resolution: to reject the racism which is its source, to give it no purchase, and when, despite everything, it obdurately persists, to fight against it mercilessly.

If one could imagine what duty the living have to the dead, I really believe that my brother could not ask for anything more.

ALSO FROM VERSO

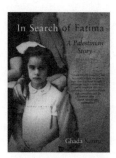

In Search Of Fatima
A Palestinian Story
GHADA KARMI

Paperback 1 85984 561 4
$16/£10/$24CAN
464 pages • 6 x 8 inches
29 b/w illustrations

'Her memoir is the story of a fascinating woman … If it is a truism to say that no one endures such a catastrophe as that of 1948 with anything except great difficulty, it is certainly not always true that special individuals can make something humanly rich and interesting out of such dire stuff.' *Edward Said*

Time Will Tell
Memoirs
YVONNE KAPP

Hardback 1 85984 510 X
$25/£15/$37CAN
328 pages • 6 x 8 inches
20 b/w illustrations

Yvonne Kapp, best known today for her biography of Eleanor Marx, was a remarkable woman whose life spanned virtually the entire twentieth century. *Time Will Tell* charts her life: 'enfant terrible' in London, the literary editor of *Vogue* in France in the late 1920s, work for anti-fascist refugee committees in 1930s' London, then, in her later years, work as a translator and a biographer.

ALSO FROM VERSO

Street Fighting Years
An Autobiography of the Sixties
TARIQ ALI

Paperback 1 84467 029 5
$17/£12.99/$25CAN
414 pages • 6 x 8 inches
43 b/w illustrations

'Tariq Ali has not lost the passion and vim which made him a symbol of the spirit of '68…
has not seen fit to join forces with the terminally cynical, or set up a graven god that can
be accused of failing … Ali has spent much of his life denouncing America as the arsenal of
counter-revolution.' *Christopher Hitchens, Observer*

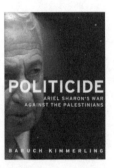

Politicide
Ariel Sharon's War Against the Palestinians
BARUCH KIMMERLING

Hardback 1 85984 517 7
$22/£15/$33CAN
240 pages • 5.5 x 7.5 inches

'Baruch Kimmerling is a brilliant and subtle thinker, who has made enormous contributions to
the understanding of Palestinian nationalism and of Israeli politics and society.' *Roane Carey, editor
of The New Intifada, and The Other Israel*

ALSO FROM VERSO

Forbidden Territory and Realms of Strife
The Memoirs of Juan Goytisolo

Paperback 1 85984 555 X
$25/£15/$37CAN
416 pages • 6 x 9 inches

'Goytisolo made sacrifices for both his literature and his politics. In a culture that now is evolved and permissive, but was then full of macho uptightness, his autobiography brought a note of total frankness.' *Edmund White*

A Civilian Occupation
The Politics of Israeli Architecture

Edited by RAFI SEGAL and EYAL WEIZMAN

Designed by David Tartakover

Hardback 1 85984 549 5
$20/£13/$30CAN
192 pages • 6 x 8.5 inches
colour and b/w illustrations

'An incriminating piece of work that shows how deeply implicated Israeli architects have been in the state's expansionism.' *Anne Karpf, Jewish Chronicle*

MORE TITLES AVAILABLE FROM VERSO

Theodor Adorno
1 84467 500 9

In Search Of Wagner
$18/£12/$25CAN

José Bové and
Francois Dufour
1 85984 405 7

The World Is Not For Sale:
Farmers Against Junk Food
$16/£10/$24CAN

Roman de la Campa
1 85984 361 1

Cuba On My Mind: Journeys to a Severed Nation
$17/£11/$25CAN

Marc Cooper
1 85984 360 3

Pinochet and Me: A Chilean Anti-Memoir
$13/£8/$19CAN

Paul Ginsborg
1 84467 541 6

Silvio Berlusconi: Television, Power and Patrimony
$16/£8.99/$23CAN

Christopher Hitchens
1 85984 398 0

The Trial of Henry Kissinger
$12/£8/$18CAN

Abdirahman A. Hussein
1 85984 390 5

Edward Said: Criticism and Society
$19/£14/$28CAN

Chalmers Johnson
1 85984 578 9

The Sorrows of Empire:
Militarism, Secrecy and the End of the Republic
£19 UK only

Annette Kuhn
1 85984 406 5

Family Secrets: Acts of Memory and Imagination
$16/£11/$24CAN

Kate Millett
1 84984 399 9

Mother Millett
$15/£10/$22CAN

Michel Surya
1 85984 822 2

Georges Bataille: An Intellectual Biography
$35/£25/$51CAN

Romila Thapar
1 84467 020 1

Somanatha: The Many Voices of A History
$25/£17/$35CAN

ALL VERSO TITLES ARE AVAILABLE FROM:

(USA) WW Norton **Tel:** 800-233-4830. Alternatively, please visit www.versobooks.com

(UK AND REST OF WORLD) Marston Book Services, Unit 160,
Milton Park, Abingdon, Oxon, OX14 4SD
Tel: +44 (0)1235 465500 / **Fax:** +44 (0)1235 465556 / **Email:** direct.order@marston.co.uk

(AUSTRALIA AND NEW ZEALAND) Palgrave Macmillan, Levels 4 & 5,
627 Chapel Street, South Yarra, Victoria 3141
Tel: 1300 135 113 / **Fax:** 1300 135 103 / **Email:** palgrave@macmillan.com.au

Macmillan New Zealand, 6 Ride Way, Albany, Auckland
Tel: (09) 414 0350 / **Fax:** (09) 414 0351

Credit cards accepted